Here's what people are saying about

How to Succeed as a Small Business Owner … and Still Have a Life

"If you own a small business, or are thinking of starting one, you need Bill Collier's wonderful book. In fact, it should be a fixture on your desk, with its pages dog-eared from use and its key points highlighted and underlined. Bill writes clearly and succinctly as a small business owner who paid his dues and learned how to do it right. That's the kind of expertise every business owner should look for in an advisor. His book is a much-needed guide for anyone who wants to get the most out of the small business experience."
- Bo Burlingham, editor-at-large of Inc. magazine and author of the book Small Giants: Companies That Choose To Be Great Instead of Big

"Bill Collier has been there and done that and provides us with helpful hints on how to take the pain out of getting there and getting it done. Bill's book clearly points out what you can do to help yourself succeed. Sometimes it takes a book to remind us what life is all about, and with a little bit of knowledge and experience how we can enjoy every minute of it. This book is such a reminder."
- Jack Stack, Founder and Chief Executive Officer of SRC Holdings Corporation, author of The Great Game of Business, and the father of the Open-Book Management movement

"This is the most practical small business book ever! I'm an avid reader/researcher and now an entrepreneur so I have read LOTS of books on small business. This is the first book that I really felt "got it!" The writer clearly knows what it is like for a small business and has realistic tips and ideas for growing your business the right way and ending up where you want it to be. This book is a MUST for every small business owner who wants to see their business grow in a sustainable way!"
- Jo Ilfeld, "The Stroller Guru", letsgostrolling.com

"How to Succeed as Small Business Owner ... and Still Have a Life has been an invaluable tool for our business. It has set our company on a pursuit to define who we are and what we want to provide for our staff, contractors and customers. The book is acting as a road map, causing us to prioritize our thoughts and actions. The change that has already taken place in our organization is exciting. We are also utilizing Bill's expertise as our business advisor. When we read Bill's book, it's like sitting across the table from him. We consider this a must read for any small business owner."
- Bob & Connie Lile, Murphy Carpet Company

"I absolutely loved Bill's book! In fact, I was so engaged that I read it in one sitting! As a business owner with two years experience, I totally related to the character in the prolog. It could have been me! Bill's insights helped me put things in perspective, organize myself differently and become more goal-oriented. I recommend any new or "semi-new" small business owner put it on their "must-read" list. Well worth the time invested in reading it!"
- Ann Grana, AMG Consulting

"How to Succeed as a Small Business Owner ... and Still Have a Life is a great read. It is truly outcome based management guided by real values and a massive dose of common sense! As I read the book and think of my business owner clients reading it too (as I will recommend), I can just imagine them nodding their heads in agreement. Well done."
- Dave Domian, LPL Financial Services

As a CPA, business advisor, and part-time accountant for a relative's business, Bill Collier's book was immensely useful.

Bill's advice to treat the business as an end to achieving your goals and not an end in itself is refreshing. He illustrates his advice with countless examples from his own experience and the experience of other entrepreneur's he's worked with.

I would recommend this book to anyone who works with, or is an entrepreneur. The book is also fantastic for anyone who has ever thought about owning a small business.
- Linda Paradis, CPA

How to Succeed as a Small Business Owner ...
and Still Have a Life!

How to Succeed

as a

Small Business

Owner ...

and Still Have a Life!

Bill Collier

Porchester Press

First Edition – 4th Printing

ISBN-10:   0-9777785-0-9
ISBN-13:   978-0-9777785-0-8

Quantity discounts are available to your company, educational institution
or organization for resale, gifts or incentive purposes. It is available
customized for banks, CPAs, attorneys, financial advisors, small business
development centers, and others with a personalized message inside the
front cover and on the front outside cover. For details, see
www.collierbiz.com.

*Dedicated to my wife Joyce, who supports me in all I do,
and to my daughters Katie and Chrissy.*

CONTENTS

Introduction

Too many small business owners work hard and don't realize above-average incomes for their risk and trouble, and many are only a few minor adjustments away from real success.

I've been there. My wife Joyce and I started our first company in the late 1980s. We distributed and serviced electronic test equipment for the medical industry, first for the local and regional marketplace and later nationally and internationally.

Like most entrepreneurs, I had done similar work for another company prior to starting this business. I got the entrepreneurial itch, and made the decision to strike out on my own when my employer - a very large company – wanted to transfer me out of town.

I wrote a business plan and got an SBA-guaranteed bank loan for $35,000. We got off to a good start: $90,000 first-year revenue, $330,000 in the second year, and $500,000 in year 3. We had decent cash flow, were at break-even or thereabouts, started hiring employees, and had a relatively easy time attracting new customers.

Then we hit a brick wall.

My lack of business expertise came home to roost. The first three years' excitement and growth turned into chaos. I was spread way too thin. I tried to be everywhere at once. The few benefits we offered employees provided no incentive for them to stay with us, so they didn't. Morale was in the gutter. Turnover was through the roof. Revenue got stuck at $500,000 for four years in a row.

I was putting in lots of hours to no avail. By the mid-1990s, I had just about had enough. I contacted one of my larger competitors about selling them my company, and was told that my little half a million dollar enterprise wasn't big enough for them to have any interest. I was discouraged beyond words.

Then, a couple of things happened.

First, I read an article about Jack Stack, his company, SRC, and open book management in Inc. Magazine. Intrigued (and maybe a bit desperate), I attended SRC's two-day session. I came home fired up about open book management. I was determined to change my company's culture, and to stem the tide of employee turnover.

The next year, a fairly good sized prospective customer in Cleveland that I'd been pursuing got bought out. The acquiring company looked like an up and coming, make-things-happen organization. A large request-for-quote came out, and I was determined to win this piece of business. I wanted it. Heck, I *needed* it.

These two events gave the company and me a much-needed shot in the arm. I felt like a long-distance runner getting his second wind.

It took several trips to Cleveland, lots of work, and some convincing of skeptics, but we won that piece of business. It turned into a long and very lucrative relationship that survived that company being bought out by a very large public firm, and the sale of my own company.

We implemented open book management, rebuilt our benefits program with input from the employees, did some strategic hiring, developed a management team and got turnover under control.

The company was on its way to a long and successful run until I sold it in early 2005. From 1995 through 2004, we enjoyed high growth, nearly zero voluntary employee turnover and terrific customer loyalty. We became ISO-9000 registered, started manufacturing many of our own products, launched an e-commerce web site, and expanded our international business to all seven continents (yes, we even shipped products to Antarctica.) We made the *St. Louis Technology Fast 50* list in 2000, 2001 and 2003 – which recognizes the fifty fastest-growing technology companies in the greater St. Louis region. In 2005, right after selling the company, I was given the *"Hall of Fame Award"* by The Great Game of Business for "extraordinary business practices and performance." We grew our revenue from $500,000 in 1994 to just a smidge under $4 million in 2004.

So, who gets the credit for this turn-around? Luck? It's been said that luck is what happens when opportunity meets preparedness, and I believe it.

Did winning that big account do it? I admit it - it certainly helped. We *won* the account by *talking*, but we *kept* the account by *doing*. Had we not performed, we would have lost it just as quickly as we won it. We did perform, kept that account and won many other big accounts over the following years.

How about open book management? OBM and the principles I learned from Jack Stack's Great Game of Business and SRC (you'll read about them later in the book) were centerpieces of our company. The openness, the sharing of information and ideas, the focus on critical metrics, the involvement of our people ... we would not have been the same company without those tenets of OBM. Even so, I can't honestly say that OBM saved the company.

I have to give my staff and management team a big portion of the credit. After I "got it" on hiring and "got it" on delegating, the turnaround started, and it was onward and upward from there. We had some good, dedicated people. It was a true team effort.

But most of the credit goes to the learning I did on the journey. This may sound like a play on words, but I'm not giving *myself* most of the credit. I'm giving it to the *ideas* I adopted along the way. Many of the ideas came from our mistakes – from trial and error. We'd do something, it wouldn't work out, and we'd try it another way. This is truly learning the hard way, as some of these lessons were expensive and painful. Some of the initiatives we implemented came from other people. I try to acknowledge the idea's source if I know it and if it appears to be that person's original idea. Then I adapt it to fit my situation or style. Hey, why reinvent the wheel?

When I was struggling and even after we righted the ship, I enjoyed learning from others – especially from more experienced and more successful entrepreneurs. As I gained experience and felt at least somewhat qualified to do so, I also enjoyed coaching and helping others with their business problems. It was this love of learning, mentoring and teaching that caused me to sell my successful company and start a new career and a new business providing coaching, consulting, speaking and training services to the small business community. It's also what drove me to write this book.

This entire book may be condensed down into three steps in your quest to succeed as a small business owner while still having a life:

- *Purpose*: Have the right attitude and mindset about business ownership (Section 1)
- *Preparation*: Have goals and a plan for achieving those goals (Section 2)
- *Execution*: Execute your plan, and perform well in specific key areas of your business (Section 3)

Simple? You bet.

Easy to accomplish? You've got to be kidding!

By the way, if you're looking for a "get rich quick" book, this isn't it. The principles I talk about in this book require hard work, dedication, persistence, patience and time.

And, if you're looking for a "get *mega*-rich" book, this isn't it. I firmly believe that owning a successful small business is the surest path to wealth in this country. But wealth, like everything else, is relative. I'm talking about an attainable level of success. Many small business owners create generational wealth but very few have it in "rock star" proportions.

This also isn't a "Hey, look at me ... look at all the extraordinary things I've accomplished!" book. That's because I believe the things I've accomplished are *not* extraordinary. I believe small business success is within the reach of most folks. Perhaps a more accurate description of my attitude would be, "Hey, look at me ... if I did it, so can you!"

You can have steady growth and improvement in your company that directly benefits you and your family. You can achieve a level of financial success, both in terms of income and net worth, virtually unobtainable in an "ordinary job." You can get into the top 5% of income in the U.S. It may not be Hilton-style wealth but it's a desirable and achievable goal. And, *you can do it while still having a life.*

Now, if you exceed these expectations and go on to become the next Bill Gates or Michael Dell ... congratulations. I'll buy *your* book.

I hope you enjoy this book, but I *really* hope you use some of the ideas to help you achieve business success and have a life.

- Bill Collier

PS - Why didn't I include a separate chapter on Open-Book Management?

As mentioned in this introduction and as you'll find out as you read on, I'm a practitioner and big fan of OBM. Yet, I didn't include a separate chapter on the subject.

Because there is an assessment that goes with the book and each chapter represents a question in that assessment. I did not want to penalize companies who do not *formally* practice OBM. OBM is addressed in various chapters, and that's almost as it should be. OBM is a subject of its own, but it also is part of communications, monitoring your numbers, and so many other segments of your business. In my mind, if you run your business in a way that includes employee education and involvement, shared risks and shared rewards, and lots of communication, then you're on the right track ... whether or not you claim to be practicing open book management.

Prolog: A week in the life of a typical frazzled and frustrated small business owner ... *It doesn't have to be this way.*

Bob is the founder and president of Bob's Printing Company, Inc. Bob learned the printing business during ten years running a press for a large family-owned printing company. When his former company was sold to an out-of-town buyer, Bob lost his job. He figured, "Hey, I know how to run a printing press. Why not be my own boss?" And so Bob's Printing Company was born. Bob's gained some business from some of his former employer's customers and enjoyed a fair amount of success early on. But soon sales reached a plateau and frustration ensued. Bob's Printing is now in its fifth year.

Monday June 29:

Bob is almost always the first to arrive and the last to leave. Today is no exception. As he unlocks the doors at 6:30AM, he looks around. He briefly remembers the feelings he had opening up during his first few months in business ... excitement and anticipation. His name was on the building and everything in the place was his – the furniture, the printing presses, the computers – even the pens in the drawers. Just as quickly as he recalled these positive emotions, they are replaced by anxiety.

Last Monday, his main press operator who had been with Bob since day one, Jeff, quit with no notice. He simply showed up at Bob's office and announced he was quitting immediately. Jeff apologized for leaving without any advance notice, but said that another opportunity came along that required him to start right away. When Bob asked Jeff about his reason for leaving, Jeff remarked that he felt disconnected from Bob and from the company. His suggestions for improvement had not been implemented, and his constructive criticism about their benefits plan had also gone nowhere. Bob was hurt by Jeff's actions and by his comments, but deep down inside Bob knew Jeff's observations were right on.

They were already behind schedule with some of Bob's most important customers. This loss of key personnel weighs heavily on Bob's mind as he makes his way to his desk, which is overflowing with stacks of papers and unopened mail. His "help wanted" ad ran in yesterday's paper, so Bob expects to start receiving resumes early this week.

Bob turns on his computer so he can check his email. His email inbox has dozens of unread messages, so he scans for important-appearing subject lines. Seeing none, he decides to fill in at Jeff's station. He's running the press when the staff begins to arrive and stays there until around noon.

After a quick lunch consisting of a bag of chips and a cup of coffee, Bob is confronted by his bookkeeper, Joan, who wants to talk about past due receivables. "Our cash flow is still a problem", explains Joan. "More than 25% of our receivables are over 60 days old." Bob knows why. Due to the relationships he had developed with his customers as he built the company during the first couple of years, Bob had made it his personal job to call and follow up on past due invoices. But things have gotten so hectic lately that he hasn't had time to make collection calls. "OK, I'll try to make some calls this week", Bob says.

Before he can even think about when he might make these calls, the company salesperson, Sally, sticks her head in Bob's office doorway. "We've got a problem. I promised the purchasing agent at Hastings Landscape that we'd deliver their brochures tomorrow. Since they gave us the job three weeks ago, this should have been plenty of time. Now I hear that it's not even on the press yet."

"I'm sorry, Sally. You know we've been behind. Our new employees aren't up to speed yet. And now, Jeff is gone, too. I'm pitching in and will get that job out for you on time." As Sally thanks Bob and turns to go, Bob follows her out and heads back out to the shop floor.

At 6:00 PM, Bob calls home to tell his wife Abby he'll be late for dinner. He finishes the Hastings job and heads out the door around 8:30. Bob gets home just in time to tuck his son and daughter into bed.

With the kids asleep, Bob and Abby have time to talk. Abby is concerned about the family's financial situation. "Bob, you haven't given yourself a raise in 18 months. And, you're not putting any money into the company retirement program."

"I know, but because of our cash flow, it just doesn't seem like a good time to take more money out of the company. I'm sure things will improve soon. Let's shoot for retirement savings and a raise starting next January."

Abby isn't satisfied with Bob's response but can tell that her husband is too tired to get into a deep discussion. She was supportive of starting the business, but five years in, Bob is only slightly above the income he made at his previous job. Abby is less concerned with Bob's income than she is with his outlook. He seems to put the company's well-being above his own. "Didn't we start this company to enhance our family's situation?" she thinks to herself.

Tuesday June 30:

Bob starts the day in his office at 7:30AM. He has intended to sort through his mail and get caught up on email for some time. He manages to make a dent in the pile of mail by 9:30 when the mail man arrives. Bob opens the mail and finds 6 resumes for the press operator job. Sorting through them, he concludes that 4 of the candidates have adequate qualifications for an interview. By noon, he manages to speak with 3 of the applicants. He sets up interviews for later today and tomorrow.

He spends the early part of the afternoon getting to the bottom of his pile of mail, but before getting to his emails it's time for his first interview. Bob greets the candidate, Larry, waits for him to fill out an application, and sits down for the interview. Bob does most of the talking, describing the company and his own background. The questions Bob asks center on the candidate's job qualifications and experience. The interview only lasts about 20 minutes.

By mid-afternoon, Bob is back in his office and finally digs into his email. He has 74 unread messages, some received as long as 10 days ago. Even though he has been scanning for important messages, he is shocked to discover that he had overlooked a message received from one of his top accounts, Brewster Manufacturing, on June 22. Brewster has been approached by one of Bob's competitors and wants Bob to send a new price quote by June 30 – today! Bob quickly calls his contact at Brewster, Linda, and gets her to agree to a one day extension on the deadline.

Brewster has been one of Bob's top revenue sources almost since day one. "How could I have missed that email?" he wonders, as he begins work on the quote. Bob could turn this job over to Sally, but Bob considers Brewster to be one of his "pet" accounts, so he tackles the job himself.

At 5:00, the phone rings. It's Bob's wife, Abby. "Where are you?" asks Abby, obviously irritated. Bob instantly realizes he has forgotten about a date he had made to meet Abby and the kids at the mall to shop for a new TV. He frantically looks for the sticky note he had on his desk as a reminder, as if it would help to find it now. "I'm so sorry, honey. Big problems with one of our top customers. How about if you gather the brochures and we'll look at them together at home later tonight?" Abby reluctantly agrees, and Bob goes back to his work on the quote. At 7:30 PM, he heads for home although some work remains.

Bob is oblivious to the fact that not only has another month ended, he's just reached the mid-year point. The first year in business, Bob eagerly anticipated the end of each month. There was usually a big push to finish the month with a bang, and every month's results were better than the one before. Now, he is simply glad to see each day end.

Wednesday July 1:

At 6:45 AM, Bob picks up where he left off the night before. He finishes the Brewster quote at 11:30 and makes the 20 minute drive to Brewster's facility. Bob drops it off, eats a fast food lunch in the car, and gets back to his office in time for his next press operator interview.

This interview goes much like the one on Tuesday. For the last two years, Sam worked for Bob's largest local competitor, Smith Printing. Bob asks Sam lots of questions about his experience there. He has little good to say about Smith and says he left over a dispute with his manager. Bob is already thinking that Sam might be able to reveal valuable information about the competition, although he came across as a bit arrogant. In fact, Sam seemed disinterested in anything about Bob's Printing other than pay and benefits.

The rest of the afternoon is spent conducting one more interview, getting caught up on mail and email, and reviewing additional resumes that came in today. Since he stood up the family last night, Bob leaves the office at 5:00 for the first time in weeks.

After dinner, Bob calls one more applicant and sets up one final interview for Thursday afternoon.

Thursday July 2:

On Thursday morning, Bob gets to the office at 7:00. On his desk is a note from Sally: "Hogan order MUST go out by noon on Thursday." Bob sighs and heads back to the shop for another day on the presses. By 2:00 PM, he gets the Hogan order finished, checks his email, and prepares for the last job applicant he has lined up.

Bob completes the interview at 4:15 and remembers the collection calls he promised to make. He makes several calls but gets nothing but voice mail. "Too late in the day to catch anyone at the office", thinks Bob. He spends another hour running the press, trying to get the workload caught up, and leaves for home at 6:00 PM.

Friday July 3:

Arriving at 7:15 AM, Bob sits down with the press applicants' resumes and his notes from the interviews. None of the candidates really impressed him, but Bob is getting tired of running the presses and being so harried. Sam, who worked at Smith Printing, had extensive printing experience and said he could start immediately. At 9:00 AM, Bob calls him to extend an offer. Sam asks a few more questions about the vacation and health insurance plans, then accepts and agrees to start next Monday morning. Bob feels a sense of relief despite his nagging doubt about Sam's "fit" in the company.

Right after lunch, Bob gets a call from Linda at Brewster. "Sorry to have to deliver bad news, but we're going to move a good chunk of our business to Johnson Printing."

Bob is stunned. "Wow! I thought we had a good relationship. Do you mind telling me how much they undercut our price?"

"Your prices are still competitive, Bob. The problem is turnaround time and general responsiveness. Our people just feel like your level of service isn't what it used to be. We'll still give you some work, but our larger jobs will be going to Johnson for the rest of this year. We'll revisit the decision in January so you'll have a chance to regain all our business. But, you'll definitely have to improve the service to have a shot at it."

Right after he finishes his conversation with Linda, Bob gets another call. It's Walter, his loan officer at the bank. "Hi, Bob. I'm just calling to remind you that your open line of credit requires you to submit monthly financials to us. We never did get the May statements. Since you're halfway through the year now, I thought I'd call and see how your year is shaping up. Have you closed the June books yet?"

Bob was caught completely flat-footed. Mixed sensations of embarrassment, anger and disappointment flood over him. He hasn't paid attention to his financials in months. He's been too busy putting out fires. "Walt, I don't think Joan has closed June yet. I'll make sure she gets those reports to you next week."

"OK. Please also have her send me the May statements as well. By the way, have her also send a copy of this year's business plan. I don't see that in your file. Have a good weekend."

Bob realizes he has dodged a bullet. He didn't answer Walter's question about his year to date results. Other than a vague idea that things must not be too bad since he has been able to make payroll and keep a little money in the bank, Bob honestly didn't know how things were going. And, he didn't have a current business plan to send. He had written a solid plan when the company started and really used it the first year. For the next year or two, things were going pretty well and the company was growing, so he just updated the original plan but didn't really refer to it. Last year, things were too hectic. By the time he even thought about planning for the new year, it was already here.

Sitting back in his chair, Bob reflects on the past week, his business and his personal life. Forgotten commitments to his family. Putting out fires. A lost customer. A frustrated salesperson, clearly losing confidence in the company. Employee turnover. A rushed hiring decision. A growing collections problem. A business without direction. An out of control schedule. Everything is a blur of activity. How did it get to be this way? How can it get better?

Section 1

PURPOSE

*Your business should serve you
... not the other way around.*

1. Why did you go into business anyway?

"I went into business because I'm passionate about my industry and about being an entrepreneur."

Hundreds of thousands of words have been written about what it means to be an "entrepreneur." Entrepreneurs have been qualified, described, classified, defined, investigated, characterized, construed, represented, delineated, designated, detailed, explained, expounded, illustrated, interpreted, and labeled. Writers have gotten into our heads, our minds, our skin and our shoes in an attempt to find out what makes entrepreneurs tick. We've been called rugged individualists, bootstrappers, risk-takers, speculators, and merchants.

I tend to use the phrase "business owner" interchangeably with "entrepreneur." In my mind, if you own all or part of a relatively small, privately held company – whether you started it, bought it, or inherited it – you fit the bill.

I'm not going to do any further defining. You know who you are and what you are. You don't need me or anyone else to tell you.

This book is written not for accomplished business owners who have taken their firms public, or who have driven their privately-held companies' revenues into the hundreds of millions of dollars. It's written for existing small to mid-sized business owners who struggle to break through to the next level ... who work hard but never seem to be able to enjoy the fruits of their labor. And it's written for future entrepreneurs, so they might avoid learning the hard way.

Before I get into *why* you started (or want to start) your business, let's spend a minute on *whether* you should have done so, or should do so in the future. (I want would-be entrepreneurs to feel included, but from now on in this book I'll refrain from referring to you, just to keep things simple. So even though things are referenced to existing business owners, it applies to you also.)

Entrepreneurship is not for everyone. I know business owners who should not be in business, and I bet you do too.

Chambers of commerce, the Small Business Administration, and the adult education departments of many community colleges sponsor "How to Start a Business" classes. If you've ever attended one of these, you've no doubt heard a litany of characteristics you need to succeed in your own business. Typically, they include things like the ability to focus on details while still watching the big picture, people skills, negotiation skills, and enough savings to keep you afloat personally until the business becomes successful enough to start paying you a salary. All these are important.

I submit to you, though, that the over-riding characteristic that separates successful entrepreneurs from also-rans is *passion*. And you need to be passionate about two things:
- **You need to be passionate about being an entrepreneur**
- **You need passion for your industry**

So, where do you get this passion? And, if you don't have it, can you get it? Beats me. I'm neither a psychologist nor a soothsayer. I don't know where it comes from, and I doubt that anyone else does, either. I doubt it can be *taught*, but maybe it can be *caught*. But I do know this: Without it, you're just going through the motions. Passion is the fuel that drives your engine. Regardless of where it comes from, you need it to succeed.

How do you know if you have a passion for something? You've heard the old saying, "If you have to ask the price, you can't afford it."

Similarly, it could be said, "If you have to ask if you're passionate about something, you probably aren't."

Think about being self-employed ... about being your own boss. Think about having your future in your own hands, a flexible schedule, financial rewards, and the potential to let your success touch others along the way.

Think about your industry, your craft, your skill.

In both cases, do you eat it, sleep it, breath it? Are you drawn to conferences and trade journals? Do you like to talk about entrepreneurship and your industry ... to share with others and learn from others? Do plans, ideas and "what ifs" pop into your head, turning themselves into written notes as soon as you get a chance?

Just to be clear, I'm not talking about obsession. If you worry that you're obsessed with business or your industry, please mark this page, put this book down and seek professional help. When you're better, start reading again right here where you left off.

Your business first serves you by feeding your passion. Some entrepreneurs may say their business completes them.

"I went into business because I'm passionate about my industry and about being an entrepreneur." Can you honestly make this statement?

> About financial rewards ... money is important. It puts food on the table, sends your kids to college, and secures your future. People do in fact get very passionate about money. But, if you go into business *just* for the money, things probably won't work out so well. Don't confuse a passion for money with passion for business or your industry. Be honest with yourself.

2. It's not "business for the sake of business"

"I believe that my business exists to serve me and to enhance the lives of my family and myself."

Too many business owners fall into a trap. And it happens all too soon. They start a company and get into a routine (you might even call it a rut.) The passion that fired them up in the first place, their families and their own needs all get shoved aside "for the sake of the business."

Don't let this happen to you. Resolve to avoid it. If it has already happened, resolve to change it.

There are demands on time. "I'd like to be out meeting new prospective customers but this order has to go out." "My spouse is going to be upset that I'm working late again, but I just can't get caught up." "Yes, business planning is important but how do I find the time?" "My staff just can't do things as well as I can, so I have to do it myself."

Then there are demands on money. "I pay my employees more than I make because the company can't afford to pay me more." "I wish I could put money into retirement funds or into savings for my kids' education, but cash flow just doesn't allow it." "I sacrifice my income for now so the company can be financially healthy."

You're not in business for the sake of being in business. You're not in business with the single-minded goal of keeping your business afloat, regardless of the impact on you and your family. There must be light at the end of the tunnel.

Remember the title of this section of the book:
Your business should serve you ... not the other way around.

This isn't just a clever slogan. You have to believe it. You have to live it.

If this was a speech instead of a book, I'd repeat it here for emphasis ...
Your business should serve you ... not the other way around.

This advice is simple, self-explanatory and unbelievably easy to violate.

Your business is a tool for enhancing your life. You'll encounter this
theme throughout this book.

Your business doesn't exist for its own sake. It exists for *your* sake. Yes,
it satisfies your passion but at the end of the day it has to pay the bills.

*"I believe that my business exists to serve me and to enhance the lives of
my family and myself."* Can you honestly make this statement?

Some folks may read "greed" into the statement *"Your
business should serve you ... not the other way around."* I'm
not espousing greed. It has nothing to do with it.

Every business has stakeholders: owners, employees, lenders,
suppliers, the community ... the list goes on. A business can
and should be operated responsibly, so that *all* stakeholders
benefit. If the idea "your business should serve you" sends up
a red flag for you, know this: Doing right by others and
benefiting from your business are *not* mutually exclusive
outcomes. In fact, it's just the opposite. The more you benefit
your stakeholders, the more successful your business will be.
We'll talk more about this in Section 3. For now, relax.

3. What if "Someday" never comes?

"I pay myself first, and don't make undue personal sacrifices of time or money for the sake of the business."

The demands on time and money are real. I imagine every small business owner has experienced it, regardless of experience or funding.

The easiest place to find time is to "borrow" it from your personal life: Longer hours, missing the kids' games, eating at the desk, or dropping out of volunteer activities.

The easiest place to find money is also to "borrow" it from your personal life: Pay yourself less (or nothing at all), put off starting a retirement fund, or even dropping important health or life insurance coverage.

These entrepreneurs generally rationalize their behavior by thinking one or more of the following:

Someday, when ...

[ ] things get better ...
[ ] I get caught up ...
[ ] we have more cash ...
[ ] I have better employees ...
[ ] the business gets bigger ...

Then I'll be able to ...

[ ] spend more time with my family.
[ ] engage in strategic planning.
[ ] make more money.
[ ] save for the future.
[ ] get back into exercising.
[ ] have a life outside the business.

How many of these have you used?

Before you scream, "Easy for you to say!" let me remind you that I've been there. I didn't come down off a mountain with these ideas on stone tablets. I ran my first company for five years before I started to "get it." It took another five years of planning and hard work – mixed with lots of trial and error – before things really turned around and started to pay off. It took me ten years to become an overnight success.

Yes, you'll have to make sacrifices when you start a business. It requires long hours, hard work, and postponing big paydays now in return for bigger paydays in the future. You need to do what needs to be done, and you need one hundred percent support from your spouse and your family.

At the same time ... don't be a martyr. And don't be a chump.

Perhaps the best way to think about a start-up is *planned sacrifice*. In other words, don't open the doors and just hope that someday you can start taking a salary. Build your salary into your plans and your projections.

That doesn't mean you should start taking a salary on day one. It also doesn't mean that you should be at any specific level of compensation. On the subject of time, it doesn't mean you shouldn't work long hours. I'm talking about a mindset, an attitude, an approach to your business in its early stages. I'm talking about the difference between winging it and planning for it.

You have to put your situation on the table and make specific decisions for yourself. If you're married and have a family, include your spouse. If your children are older, including them in the discussion will be a good learning experience for them, too. Ask questions like:

- How long are we able and willing to go without an income after start-up?
- What level of salary is desired and/or needed after 1 year, 2 years, and 5 years?
- What insurance coverages do we need, and how will we pay for them?
- What hours can I work and still meet our family's needs?
- What leisure activities am I willing to put aside for a while?

Notice that the statement we're discussing in this chapter doesn't say *"... I don't make personal sacrifices of time or money..."* It says *"... I don't make <u>undue</u> personal sacrifices..."* Let's explore this idea of "undue" sacrifices.

Some synonyms for "undue" include excessive, unreasonable, extreme, and inappropriate. If one of these words helps drive the point home for you, great. Just be sure you go into business with both eyes open. Map out your time and money requirements, expect and plan for sacrifice, and don't get sucked into martyrdom.

We'll talk about personal planning in the next section. For now, I hope you buy into the idea that paying yourself first needs to be part of the planning process, for both your personal plans and your business plans. It's an important part of the "your business serves you" concept.

When your enterprise can afford it, budget for a fair rate of pay for yourself. Work it into a regular payroll schedule – preferably weekly or bi-weekly. Don't leave it to chance or "if there's enough left over after paying the bills." Your pay should become an obligation of the company, just like paying other employees, paying taxes, and paying your vendors.

Trade-offs are a way of life for entrepreneurs. Your compensation is part of a trade-off between leaving cash in the company to finance current liquidity and future growth, and your personal prosperity. If your company has reached a point of relative success, your own pay should at least be comparable to the amount you'd need to pay a competent and qualified "hired hand" to run your operation. More pay can come with increased business success, but don't get greedy. Think long-term.

"I pay myself first, and I don't make undue personal sacrifices of time or money for the sake of the business." Can you honestly make this statement?

Section 2

PREPARATION

If you don't know where you're going, any road will take you there.

4. The Basics of Goal-Setting and Planning

"I set goals that are specific, ambitious, achievable and balanced. I define tasks & action steps for each one."

Goals

Goals should be Specific, Ambitious, Achievable, and Balanced. Think of the automobile brand SAAB to help you remember. Aim for the top 5%.

Specific: "Making lots of money" isn't specific. "Earning $200,000 per year within 6 years of starting my company" is. "Living in a nice house" isn't specific. "Owning a 4,000 square foot home in a gated golf community before my 50th birthday" is. "A short work week" may mean 30 hours to one person but 50 to another. Be specific as to outcome and timeframe.

Ambitious and Achievable: At first glance, these two words may seem to be in conflict with one another. However, I prefer to think of them as complementary. I see the dual concepts of ambitious and achievable as "safety valves" for your goal-setting. It doesn't make sense to pick goals that are very easy to achieve, nor should you bother to set goals that are impossible to reach. Set the bar high ... but not too high!

Balanced: To be sure, monetary goals are important. But, don't spend so much time thinking about the things money will buy that you ignore the important things money can't buy. Balance your goal-setting among all the aspects of your present life and future life: your kids' education, time off from work, vacations, health, extended family, and so on. The same goes for your business goals. Don't just focus on revenue or growth. Consider goals for quality, employee satisfaction and other important facets of your company. Just to be clear ... the idea is not to build balance into *each individual goal*. Strive for balance when you look at *all of your goals in total*.

If you do any reading at all on the subject of goals, you'll quickly discover the acronym SMART goals. SMART stands for specific, measurable, achievable, realistic and tangible. I think it's a lot to remember, and I also think we should keep the concept of "balance" in mind when setting goals. But, if the SMART approach works better for you, great ... as long as you're setting goals and then proactively working toward their achievement.

Aim for the top 5%: I came across this idea years ago in a motivational audio tape set called "Lead the Field" by Earl Nightingale. In it, Mr. Nightingale encourages the listener to shoot for the top 5% in everything you do. The idea stuck with me, and I've incorporated it into much of my own life. Specific goals are good, but what if you don't know where you want to go? This "top 5%" concept worked for me. Let's take your family's income as an example. According to the U.S. Census Bureau, the top 5% family income bracket for 2004 (the most recent data available as of this writing) starts at $157,176. Achieve it, and you've joined the Top 5% of U.S. households in terms of income. Again, Warren Buffett you're not, but put it in perspective. Where was your income before you started your business? Getting into the Top 5% of income earners is a significant step up for most entrepreneurs. And, you can use this same approach for almost any aspect of personal or business planning: the top 5% in customer satisfaction, the top 5% of home values in your community ... you get the idea. It's a simple yet ambitious goal.

Planning

Start with a goal and work backwards from there to define the tasks and action steps needed on a yearly, monthly, weekly and daily basis that will move you toward your goal. (A goal without a plan for achieving it is just a dream.)

Here's an example:

Your goal is for you and your spouse to take a ten day vacation to Branson, Missouri. You plan to drive there, and you want to go between Thanksgiving and Christmas. You have a budget of $2,500. (Note that this is a specific goal.)

As you go about planning to achieve this goal, you'll have a series of tasks that need to be accomplished, and each task will have action steps associated with it.

One task will be to make hotel reservations. The action steps associated with this task might be to:
1.   Visit the Branson Chamber of Commerce website to research hotels
2.   Check location, availability, amenities and prices
3.   Choose a hotel
4.   Call to reserve the room

The sequence was: **Goals > Tasks > Action Steps**

Most people would consider "Make hotel reservation" a to-do. But you can see from this example that it really is a task that needs to be broken down into smaller action steps. You'll find that most of the goals you want to accomplish – both personal and business - are made up of intermediate tasks, which in turn are made up of action items.

Let's expand the sequence:

The Goal-Setting & Planning Model	
Long-Term Vision	The "Big Picture" ... specific goals and targets combined with descriptions.
3-5 Year Vision	Where I want and need to be in 3-5 years, to keep me on track toward my long-range vision.
Strategies	The overall approaches you'll use in pursuit of your goals
1 Year Goals and Targets	Intermediate goals and targets that move you toward your 3-5 year Vision.
Tasks	Think of these as "projects." The specific accomplishments that contribute to achieving the 1 Year Goals.
Action Steps	Think of these as "to-do" items. This is the daily and weekly nitty-gritty work. It's where the rubber meets the road.

As you move from long-term toward present day, your thinking becomes increasingly less strategic and more tactical. Let's explore the difference.

Strategies are your long-term, overall plans and approaches for achieving your goals.
Tactics are the short-term, specific actions you take as defined by your strategy.

For example, your <u>strategy</u> for making the most of your retirement funds might be to invest in no-load mutual funds. Some of the <u>tactical</u> moves you'd make – consistent with your strategy – would be the purchase of specific funds.

Another example: Your <u>strategy</u> for growing your company's sales might include exhibiting at trade shows. The <u>tactic</u> associated with this strategy would be to exhibit at a specific show.

"I set goals that are specific, ambitious, achievable and balanced. I define tasks & action steps for each one." Can you honestly make this statement?

5. First, Personal and Family Goals

"I have personal & family goals: long-term, short-term, retirement & multi-generational."

For your business to serve you, it makes sense that you first have to define what "serving you" means. Giving thought to your personal and family goals, and ideally, putting them down in writing, is the first step.

Few couples will write up a formal plan for their future. Some will find the exercise cold and calculating, reducing their hopes and dreams to bullet points on a page. Others will find it hard to devote time to the effort. Your spouse - if less goal-oriented than you - may find the very idea silly. If any of these descriptions fits you, don't worry. You won't need a fancy document or Power Point presentation. Nobody else will even see it.

But, it is important for all couples – especially business-owning couples – to talk about the future. Do the husband and wife have similar aspirations? Do both spouses want to work in the company? When will retirement happen? Will the children take over the family business? If not, who will?

These and dozens of other questions need to be discussed. You don't need a detailed response to each (although it wouldn't hurt), but strive for at least a general understanding of your common plans and goals. Wide differences deserve special attention and enough discussion and compromising to narrow the gap to a level acceptable to both.

Determine the most important concerns and write them down. Again, nothing fancy ... just get your thoughts on paper. Once you've done it, I recommend you pull it out once a year or so and revisit your list. People change. Circumstances change. Opportunities come and go. Of course your list will need to be updated periodically. The result of this important work can serve two purposes. First and foremost, it can help a couple communicate and set goals – important for any family with or without a business. Second, it lays the groundwork for a business whose plans are in concert with the personal plans of the owners.

If you're single, of course, you can disregard all this stuff about couples and families. But you should still have a personal plan.

Here are some of the goals to be included in your personal plan:

- **Long-range goals (3-5 years or more)**
- **Short-term goals (One year out)**
- **Retirement goals**
- **Multi-generational goals**

Depending on your age and other factors, you may or may not have a clear vision for some of these. For instance, if you aren't yet married it will be difficult – maybe impossible – to envision retirement or multi-generational goals. That's OK, and it's why I recommend you revisit and update your plans once in a while.

Long-Range Goals – 3-5 Years or More

How much money do you want to earn down the road? How many hours per week will you want to work? Where will you want to live? When will you want to pay off your mortgage? Will your kids attend public, private, or parochial schools? Or, will they be home schooled? What colleges will they attend? Do you need to budget for your children's weddings? Will other family members be involved in your business? Will you start a second company? What leisure and family activities will you want to engage in? How about volunteering and charitable giving? Don't forget vacations, investments, and other aspects of your future life.

Short-Term Goals – One Year Out

Remember what we covered in Chapter 4, on goal-setting and planning? Each of your long-term goals should have shorter-term, intermediate goals (tasks) assigned that move you toward your long-term goals.

You may also have some goals that are, by definition, short-term. These are goals that come and go within a one year period. For instance, you may have a goal to replace your car. Chances are, you'll be planning for an event like this within a year. Consider how many hours you want to work per week and what sort of personal income you want within the next year.

Retirement Goals

When you get older, retirement begins to loom. Don't wait too long to plan for it. This plays a vital role in your "End Game" planning for your business. Will you plan to sell to a partner, an employee, or a third party? Or, will you want to pass the company along to your kids? Will you want a lump sum buyout, or payments over time? What sort of retirement lifestyle and income do you want? Don't forget to account for inflation when running the numbers!

Multi-Generational Goals

If you have children, you'll want to consider how to work them into your estate plan. Maybe they'll have a role in business succession. Perhaps you'll even provide for grandchildren and great-grandchildren via a trust or other estate planning vehicle.

"I have personal & family goals: long-term, short-term, retirement & multi-generational." Can you honestly make this statement?

6. Then, Business Goals

"I have business goals: long-term, short-term and an exit strategy. All are consistent with my personal goals."

Your business goals must be created in alignment with your personal goals, since your business exists to serve you and to enhance your life. Whatever your personal income goal, clearly the business must throw off enough cash to pay you. The same applies to personal goals related to long-term wealth accumulation, time off, retirement, and so on: Your business goals must be in concert with your personal goals.

So many business owners pick arbitrary goals with nary a thought to the impact on their personal lives. "I want to be at ten million in revenue within 5 years." Or, "Twenty-five percent annual growth is my target." All well and good, but shouldn't the *real* goal be to use the business as a tool to serve you and your family ... to enhance your personal life? If getting to ten million in sales or twenty-five percent growth requires 60 hour workweeks and half of your time on the road away from your family, is it worth it?

Let's say your personal income target is $175,000 per year. If you can achieve that level of income with a $3 million business, why endure the headaches and additional potential liabilities associated with a bigger company?

On the other hand, if a family-owned business intends to support the founders, several of their children, plus the children's spouses with jobs and incomes, that clearly will require a significant enterprise.

Aside from monetary considerations, you may have personal aspirations to spend lots of quality time with your spouse and your kids, or to get involved in community organizations, take up a hobby, start a second business, or any other number of things that require ample leisure time. If so, a hard-charging, fast-growth business model may be contrary to your personal goals.

This chapter is about business goals, but I am intentionally revisiting the information we covered in the previous chapter. Think things through and discuss your business plans with your spouse. Today's business success can become tomorrow's family regret. Don't become a servant to the business, and don't send the business in a direction that doesn't move you toward your personal goals.

Long-Term Vision

The further out you're looking, the more "big picture" you need to be. Think beyond simple numbers and ratios. What is your long-range vision for your company? To be the leader in your industry, in your town, in your state, or in the entire country? To have a trusted management team in place, freeing you up for other endeavors? To sell the company in ten years for five million dollars?

Short-Term Goals

Your long-range thinking will have a dramatic impact on your short-term goals because, as we've discussed, the way to accomplish long-term goals is to work backward: Intermediate steps toward your long-range goals help define your short-term goals.

Additionally, you may have some specific short-term goals for your business related to your personal goals. For example, You may want to adjust your working hours, your travel schedule, or your own pay for the next year.

The End Game

Your personal plan should include your goals for eventually exiting the business. I can't tell you how sorry I feel for company owners who decide to simply shut their doors and retire. They have a small sale and get rid of their desks and other equipment for pennies on the dollar. Why didn't they anticipate and prepare for this event by making it desirable to potential buyers? Don't let this happen to you.

As you progress through your years as a business owner, concentrate on building value into your company. There are few opportunities in life to build greater wealth than via business ownership.

Your exit strategy comes into play *before* you even form your business. Choosing the right entity type up front (corporation, sub-chapter S corporation, LLC, etc.) plays a major role in how heavily your proceeds from an eventual sale will be taxed. Seek the advice of a good CPA/tax advisor when making this critical decision.

"I have business goals: long-term, short-term and an exit strategy. All are consistent with my personal goals." Can you honestly make this statement?

7. High-falutin' business plans for bankers, the SBA and outside investors; a *real* business plan for you

"I have a written business plan with a vision, strategies, a budget & an action plan for achieving all these."

There are only two circumstances where I recommend a long, detailed business plan with lots of paragraphs of prose:

1. If you are seeking outside loans or investments. Your funding source will almost certainly require plenty of detailed information, which allows them not only to learn about your industry, but also to gauge how well you understand your business.
2. When you are planning a start-up. The process of sorting through and writing down your issues, concerns, goals, plans, and numbers will help crystallize your thoughts.

Some of the information that you might include in such a plan: Background on your industry, your own biography, a list of key competitors, barriers to entry, demographic info, list of suppliers, an organizational chart, and so on.

But, if you and your staff need to read through pages of embellishments to get to the part that says "Our revenue target this year is $1 million" ... well, I can tell you from personal experience that plan will be left in a drawer.

For your own day-to-day use, your business plan is a working document that covers one year. By the end of the year, it should be worn and dog-eared. For it to be useful as a working document, it should be as brief as possible. Think bullet points rather than prose.

Your working plan should fit on 6 or so pages. That includes:

- The main business plan. 1 or 2 pages
- Your budget ... at minimum: income statement, balance sheet, and cash flow projections. 3+ pages.
- Marketing Plan. 1 page. (Covered in next chapter.)

The Components of the Business Plan

Mission Statement: This defines your main products and services. This is not a flamboyant, high-minded statement to be hung on the wall or posted on your website. (You may want one of those. That's OK. But that's not what this is.) This is a simple statement of what you do. It serves as a reminder to you and your staff ... to help you stay on track and "keep you between the guardrails."

Primary market/customer base: Demographic, geographic, industry, etc.
Secondary markets: Demographic, geographic, industry, etc.
Your target market is not "anyone with money." Trying to be all things to all customers is a formula for failure.

What values and principles are important to the company: Examples: Integrity, customer service, quality, and respect. Chapter 11 is entirely dedicated to this subject.

Unique Selling Proposition: This answers the question "Why should customers buy from you instead of your competition?" Your USP is vitally important. It tells a customer specifically and clearly why you're the best choice. "We provide excellent service" is not a USP. If your competitor can make the same claim, it isn't unique. You may even have to tweak your business model to develop a USP. Keep it brief! Most importantly, *make sure it is relevant and important to your targeted customer base!* For instance, a pharmacy owner in a community of busy young families might need to make "speedy service" part of the USP, while a similar pharmacy in a retirement community may need to emphasize "personalized assistance with prescriptions." A prospective customer's response to your USP should not be "So what?", and it also should not be "Yeah, right. Everyone makes that claim." Think *unique* and *relevant*.

Strengths, Weaknesses, Opportunities, & Threats: Pretty much self-explanatory. Strengths and weaknesses are internal; opportunities and threats are external. Keep the ego in check and *be brutally honest*.

3 Year Vision: Your 3 Year Vision comes from the long-term vision you have for the business. It answers the question, "Where does this company need to be in 3 years to keep it on track toward its long-range vision?" Example: "By the end of 2010, this will be a $5 million business with solid profitability and cash flow. We will have three locations and will be the regional leader in our industry." Use specific goals but also let your passion show through. Create a compelling, inspiring vision for you and your team. I recommend looking out 3 years, but you may choose to work from a 5 year vision or some other timeframe.

1 Year Targets: These are specific financial measures that you need to hit in the new year to keep you on track toward your 3 Year Vision. These should at least include revenue, and can include profit or other key "measurables." Example: Let's say you did $3.5 million last year, and your 3 Year Vision calls for $5 million in revenue. Your 1 Year Target might call for growing to $4.2 million. This should just be a brief "bullet-point" list of important measures. Your budget will cover all the numbers in detail, and you'll track your progress throughout the year using your Key Performance Indicator report (chapter 18.)

Strategies:
What marketing, sales, management and other strategies will you use to reach your vision? These are general statements that describe the approaches you'll use. Examples:
- Aggressive local advertising campaign
- E-Commerce
- Improve profitability by increasing Gross Margins and Revenue/Employee
- Improve cash position via faster collections
- Pay our employees at or above industry average
- Keep our prices on par with local competitors

1 Year Goals:
These are the specific goals or initiatives that are to be accomplished this year. They flow from your 3 Year Vision, your 1 Year Targets, and your Strategies. Example:

Goal 1: **Launch E-Commerce Website & make 5%** of revenue online		Due: **End of year**
Task 1: **Choose e-commerce vendor & software**	Owner: **JB**	Due: **1/31**
Task 2: **Trial/Beta testing of web store**	Owner: **JB**	Due: **3/25**
Task 3: **Go live with online store**	Owner: **JB**	Due: **4/10**
Task 4: **Marketing campaign to drive traffic to online store**	Owner: **TD**	Due: **4/22**
Goal 2: **Open 2nd location**		Due: **9/30**
Task 1: **Complete demographic study & choose zip code for new location**	Owner: **GR**	Due: **3/30**
Task 2: **Choose commercial real estate agent**	Owner: **LK**	Due: **4/15**
Task 3: **Identify property and negotiate lease**	Owner: **LK**	Due: **6/1**
Task 4: **Buy fixtures and equipment**	Owner: **SD**	Due: **7/15**
Task 5: **Hire & train new staff, plan for grand opening**	Owner: **LK**	Due: **9/30**

Each Task (you can think of these as "projects") should have its own separate page, where it is broken down into action steps, each with a timeframe and accountability assigned to a specific person. These separate Task pages aren't really part of the business plan. It is delegated and assigned work. This is a distinction worth making to the person responsible for the task. At that level, it's not "just a plan." It is specific work that needs to be completed per the assigned and agreed-upon timeframe.

Be realistic! Yes, you should be optimistic. I wrote earlier that your goals should be ambitious, and I stand by that advice. But I also advised that your goals should be achievable. If for next year you plan to rebuild your benefits plan from scratch, move to a new location, gain ISO-9002 certification, and grow by 50% - all I can tell you is "good luck." It sounds like a formula for disappointment. There is a benefit – especially when you first start doing business planning – to choose relatively conservative goals. Get some successes under your belt, celebrate with your team, and get used to achieving your goals. Then you can get more aggressive. Remember, Rome wasn't built in a day.

Constantly challenge all your annual, monthly, weekly and daily activities by asking, "Is this moving us toward our long-range vision?"

Choosing realistic 3 year and 1 year targets

Once you know where you want to be a 3 years out, you can work backward from there to get to your one-year targets.

For instance, let's say you're a start-up. Your specific, balanced, ambitious, achievable and personally-aligned goal is to hit $750,000 in revenue in your third year. Do you think you'll ramp up quickly in years one and two, and level off in year three? Or, will year one be a slow build-up, with more rapid growth in years two and three? Nobody can answer that for you. You'll have to consider your industry, the competition, customer demand, your available resources, and a hundred other factors.

After careful consideration of all the information you can gather, you decide you can do $250,000 in year one, double to $500,000 in year two, and grow to $750,000 in year three.

Another potential outcome: You determine there's no way you can grow fast enough in three years to get to $750,000, and so you re-calibrate your targets.

Either way, you can see how working backward gives you some perspective on the in-between years, and on how achievable and realistic your goals are.

The Budget

You should have your management team deeply involved in the budget process. The sales department should make its own revenue projections. Other departments should set targets for their expenses. Don't do it all by yourself, and don't let the accounting department do it. Get the appropriate folks involved, and take the time needed to educate all of them so they understand what the numbers mean, how the financials interact, and how each department and employee impacts the numbers. As mentioned elsewhere in this book, you may find that you need to send some of your management team members to an accounting class.
Your annual budget includes an income statement (also called a Profit and Loss statement, or P&L), a balance sheet and a cash flow statement.

All are educated guesses of what will happen, based on your past performance and your knowledge of facts related to your company: the competition, new products, your customers, the industry, the economy, your staff, and so on. Don't work up a budget in a vacuum. Find out what's going on both inside and outside of your company.

As you work on your budget projections, use your time and effort wisely. For instance, one of your largest expenses may be cost of goods sold. By negotiating with suppliers and/or controlling waste, you think you can reduce this number from 30% of revenue down to 25%, and thus send tens of thousands of extra dollars straight to the bottom line. If so, then of course this number deserves much of your attention. However, let's say one of your overhead expense line items is "City Business License", and you have to renew each year for $25. Will the city raise it next year to $30? *Who cares?* Don't waste a single second agonizing over it. The number is so small and insignificant that you should simply throw a number in that space and move on! I'm not promoting sloppy budgeting ... I am promoting that you leverage your limited time by concentrating on areas of significance and areas where you can actually impact the outcome.

Your first couple of budgets may be wildly off. Don't stop doing it. Projecting your numbers is something that you'll get better at as time goes on.

Once you work up a budget, how will you actually use it? Your budget helps you make critical business decision about things like hiring, benefits, capital equipment expenditures, facilities ... literally everything you do is dependent on having a well-thought-out budget. Your business plan contains action steps for hitting these targets, and the chapter on Key Performance Indicators will tell you how to monitor your progress.

Income Statement

If you don't want to work up a complete, detailed income statement – although I recommend you do – at least include the following categories:

	Revenue (categorized as appropriate)
Less	**Cost of Goods Sold (COGS)**
Equals	**Gross Margin**

	Overhead Expense, consisting of:
Less	Compensation-related expenses
	Sales & Marketing expenses
	Other overhead expenses (categorized as appropriate)
Equals	**Net Profit Before Tax**

Resist the temptation to simply take a number from the prior year and add for inflation. Instead, use *zero-based budgeting*. This approach assumes that each budget number must be justified starting at zero, and last year's results have little bearing on the new year's target amount.

Balance Sheet and Cash Flow Statement

These two reports show, among other things, a critical factor: How much cash you have to work with. If you don't do anything else – *do not run out of cash.*

Another very important number: Accounts receivable. You may have a great sales year, but if you can't collect, you're in trouble.

The balance sheet is a snapshot in time of your financial position: assets, liabilities and equity. For budgeting and planning purposes, project your starting and ending balance sheet numbers.

The cash flow statement, as its name implies, shows inbound and outbound cash flows.

Many small companies focus on the income statement and virtually ignore the balance sheet and cash flow statement. Admittedly, the income statement is where the action is. Everyone wants to talk about sales and profits. Here's another angle on the matter for you to consider:

While it's exciting to see sales and profits rolling in, those two measures are really just the means to an end. The real deal – the big payoff – is *equity*. The equity in your business is part of your own personal net worth, assuming you own the company. For me, the big thrill is to take a look at personal net worth and see it growing from year to year. If you own the business, the company equity is part of your personal net worth.

So, spend time projecting your income statement numbers ... *and* give these other statements an appropriate amount of attention.

The Last Word on Business Planning and Budgeting

Having a plan and a budget is important. *Creating* a plan and a budget is even more important. Sound like double-talk? Here's what I mean.

The *process* you go through to create your plans – deep thinking, discussions, disagreements, calculations, research – is much more valuable than the finished document that results. This proactive strategic planning work will benefit you and your business in uncountable ways.

Please don't conjure up a business plan on your own and then present it to your staff. (Even worse: writing your own plan and then keeping it to yourself.) If you want to succeed, tap into the collective brainpower of your management team and even your rank and file employees. Get their input. The opportunities for good things abound during the strategic planning process ... developing employees, creating excitement, showing trust, creating buy-in, finding out what your people are thinking ... the list goes on.

U.S. general and president Dwight D. Eisenhower said, "Plans are nothing; planning is everything."

Professional baseball player Roger Maris said, "You win not by chance, but by preparation."

"I have a written business plan with a vision, strategies, a budget & an action plan for achieving all these." Can you honestly make this statement?

8. Marketing plans

"I have and use written marketing plans and a marketing budget."

Just as with your business plan, let's make a distinction between a grandiose, long marketing plan and a *working* marketing plan. (By now you can guess which one I favor.) Stick with the nuts and bolts. We're going to discuss a no-fluff marketing plan.

For me, a marketing plan is a no-compromise situation. You simply *must* have one. I'll give you three reasons: Focus, effectiveness and money.

Without going through the exercise of analyzing your target market and how to best get your message to them, you're spinning your wheels. Rather than focusing your efforts on an effective message being sent via well-planned media and well-thought-out approaches, you'll go through the year bouncing from one marketing vehicle to another. You'll be an easy target for every salesperson hawking newspaper ads, magazine ads, radio ads, web links, ads in school play programs, coupon mailers and banners being towed behind airplanes. "This will boost your sales!" they'll all claim. Of course, not one of them will guarantee that responses or sales leads will come your way as a result. (Unlike your ad salesperson, I am fully prepared to provide you with an iron-clad guarantee related to their services, and I will stand behind it. Here it is: Your ad dollars *will* reduce your bank account balance. I guarantee it.)

It is easy to run willy-nilly between every marketing and advertising opportunity that comes along. Throwing good money into paid advertising is something many companies do in an effort to boost sales, often with disappointing results.

In my mind, your marketing plan is almost more important for defining what marketing activities you *won't* do than what you *will* do. You and your team should spend the requisite time to think through the process, set a budget, and then execute it. Of course you may need to make some minor adjustments mid-year, but don't wildly veer off course. If you really did your homework and dug into it, you will have chosen an appropriate message and appropriate approaches to get that message to your intended audience. Don't scrap your plan just because the phone isn't ringing off the hook – especially early in your campaign. Give it time to work. You should resist the temptation to throw money at marketing. Your marketing plan helps you resist that temptation. Stick to your plan.

In fact, just as a cross wards off vampires, your marketing plan can ward off blood-sucking ad salespersons. "Sorry, my plan and budget are both set for the entire year. Maybe next year."

OK, we've established the fact that you need a plan. How do you come up with one?

To get started, here are some pearls of wisdom for you to consider:

- Design a sales and marketing mix appropriate for your business. Measure results and make adjustments as needed.
- Focus portions of your promotion strategy on all of the following: gaining new customers, keeping existing customers, and growing your business with existing customers.
- *Everyone* in the company is responsible for attracting and retaining customers!
- Put your customers to work for you ... testimonials and referrals are powerful and free.
- Develop relationships with your customers and become a valuable resource for them. Remember: People buy from people.
- Consistency and repetition are the keys to effective marketing and branding. Beware of any practices that would take away from your brand and identity.

Another term for marketing is Lead Generation. Any active or passive activity that generates leads is marketing, and you should employ a well-rounded assortment of active and passive, and both free and paid-for, marketing activities.

Here are some of the types of things you might consider:

- Website
- Email newsletter
- Print newsletter
- Community and service organization memberships
- Trade association memberships
- Newspaper articles about your company
- Get interviewed on radio or TV
- Radio or TV stories about your company
- Signage and banners on your facility
- Billboards
- Print advertising
- Press releases
- Direct mailing
- Yellow Pages listing
- Donate products to auction fundraisers
- Customer endorsements/testimonials
- Referrals and word-of-mouth
- Contests/drawings/promotions
- Event sponsorships
- Tradeshows
- Speak/present in educational sessions at symposiums and conferences

I strongly recommend that you have both a marketing plan and a budget to go with it. Your plan should include ongoing, simultaneous monthly activities from multiple marketing categories.

A simple spreadsheet can meet your need for both a plan and a budget. Here's an example, showing just the first quarter of the year:

	January	February	March	Total
Magazine Ad	$250	$250	$250	$750
Direct Mailing	$600	---	$600	$1200
Trade Show	---	$1500	---	$1500
Email Newsletter	$0	$0	$0	$0
Total	$850	$1750	$850	$3450

Look at all the information it packs:
- First, you are able to plug in all the various marketing activities you want to engage in – whether they cost money or not. Remember,

you're doing this not just for the budget numbers, but also to schedule and plan your activities. My personal preference is to use some hyphens to illustrate that there is no activity in that category for the month. Showing "$0" in a space means that the activity is happening, but there is no cost associated with it. Put *something* in every space to avoid confusion.

- The numbers across the bottom give your total marketing budget for each month.
- The numbers down the far right column give your total marketing budget for each category.
- The number at bottom right is your total overall marketing budget for the year.

In a real-life scenario, you wouldn't just say "Magazine Ad." You'd say specifically what ad, what size, color or black/white, and what magazine. You'd put in as much detailed information as needed to guide you through budgeting, planning and implementation.

Once you and your team have worked up your plan and budget, you have to implement it, track it, and tweak it.

First and most importantly, make someone individually responsible for turning your marketing plan into action. You can split the duties up, but each facet of the plan must have one specific person in charge of making his or her piece happen on time and on budget.

Tracking and measuring marketing results is important, but is admittedly difficult. That's why most small companies don't measure the performance of their marketing efforts. Here are a few tricks you can use to try to quantify your return on marketing dollars:

- Ask! Ask every caller how they found out about your company, or if they saw a certain ad. Use a simple notepad and tick marks to count callers who say they are responding to your current marketing efforts. Your sales department can also track sales results from these callers.
- Do written, web, in-store or phone surveys of customers. Ask questions about your marketing campaigns: "Have you seen this ad?" "Did it get your attention?" "Was the message compelling?"
- Use a special email address, web site, or phone number in an ad. Or, tell customers in your marketing piece to ask for a specific offer. Count both the number of responses and the sales dollars that result.

- Use software to measure visitor traffic to your website.
- Require the customer to cut out your ad or a coupon to take advantage of your offer.
- Count the number of visitors to your store or facility.

It will take some thought and creativity, but you can and should come up with ways to track and measure your marketing effectiveness.

Finally, be willing to tweak your plans. This gets tricky, because there may be a fine line between stopping a campaign before it had a real chance to get traction, and hanging on too long with a losing approach. That's why research, planning and measurement are all so important. So, be smart and don't be stubborn. If, despite your best efforts, a certain marketing approach is clearly not yielding results, make a change and learn from the experience.

"I have and use written marketing plans and a marketing budget." Can you honestly make this statement?

9. Plan your work, then work your plan.

"I actively use my plans to run my business. I review them periodically & change course when appropriate."

"The man who does not read good books has no advantage over the man who cannot read them."

"The business owner who has plans but does not use them has no advantage over the business owner who has no plans."

One of these two quotes is from Mark Twain. The other is from me. Can you guess which is which?

Having your plan is a good start. *Executing* your plan separates winners from also-rans. It is the difference between success and just getting by.

There is simply no substitute for action. Poorly-planned action will outdo well-planned inactivity every time.
Here is one of my favorite sayings: "Do *something*, even if it's wrong."

This chapter is short and sweet. It is simply – and literally – a call to action.

You *must* keep your goals and plans front and center, and literally use them to drive your activities. This requires a tremendous amount of discipline and a sense of urgency. Since entrepreneurs are generally not accountable to anyone but themselves, it is easy for most of us to slip into bad habits and to let plans slide.

If you don't have the discipline required to execute your plans, you need to put some sort of mechanism in place to keep you on track. You and your management team should hold each other accountable for execution and results. Make sure they know it's OK to call you out when you drop the ball, with no fear of reprisal. Or, it might be a mentor ... a fellow entrepreneur or group of entrepreneurs, with whom you meet periodically to review your progress. It might be an advisory board of trusted advisors you assemble. (I'd avoid putting my banker or attorney in that group, by the way.) Maybe your spouse can help. I'll make an unabashed pitch for consultants and coaches like me at this point. (Hey, it's my book!) Basically, find *someone* to "hold your feet to the fire."

You should review your plan frequently and be willing to make adjustments. Similar to the advice I gave in the previous chapter on tweaking your marketing plans mid-stream, don't jettison your plan at the first sign of trouble. Be willing to stick with it and give it a chance to work. After all, you're smart, you dug in and gave your plans due time and attention, you're passionate about the desired results, and you involved others in crafting your plans. Later in the book we'll cover Key Performance Indicators which will provide forward-looking measures to help avoid problems. But even with diligent use of tools like this, some hiccups are inevitable. Perhaps the best advice is to avoid impulsive behavior. Think things through and consider all your options. Then, if it seems like a reasonable and rational response, go ahead and change your plans - and learn from the experience.

"I actively use my plans to run my business. I review them periodically & change course when appropriate." Can you honestly make this statement?

Section 3

EXECUTION

If you put in long hours, have trouble getting away from work for more than a day or two at a time, and don't make any more money than you did when you worked for someone else, you haven't created a business. You've created a job.

10. Make optimum use of your time

"I make good use of time. I use a calendar, and I schedule personal time and planning time for myself".

What do you have in common with Donald Trump?

Question: What do you have in common with Donald Trump?
Answer: You both get 24 hours per day.

You may or may not admire Donald Trump, but you have to admit that his business accomplishments are of heroic proportions. Everything he's done has happened within the same time constraint that you and I are stuck with: There are only 24 hours in a day.

Think of all the people of accomplishment, past and present. Leonardo da Vinci. Thomas Jefferson. Mother Teresa. Thomas Edison. Condoleezza Rice. Bill Gates. Margaret Thatcher. Tiger Woods. Billy Graham. Pope John Paul II. Your grandparents. Your parents. The person you admire most – whoever that may be.

Every single accomplishment ... in business, politics, the arts, medicine, science ... in peacetime or in war ... long ago or in modern times ... has been achieved by someone who only had 24 hours in each day. No more.

If anything could be called a "great equalizer", it would be time. We all get the same amount of time each day. It's not how much time we *get*. It's all about what we *do* with the time we get.

So, the next time you are tempted to excuse a lack of results with "There aren't enough hours in the day", stop and think about what others do with their daily allotment of time.

Know when to say "Yes" and when to say "No"

The phrase "time management" has become a cliché. And in case you haven't noticed, I use more clichés than you can shake a stick at. So, in the interest of staying under the cliché quota, let's briefly talk instead about *self*-management. In fact, it would be appropriate to call it *life* management.

As an entrepreneur, you have the extraordinary opportunity to be in complete control of your schedule and over which activities you will (and won't) be engaged. So, it's critically important to know when to say "yes" and when to say "no."

You have the ability to say "yes" to the people and issues that matter most. Unfortunately – and here's where many of us get into trouble – you also have the ability to say "yes" to the people and issues that matter least.

This is why the things we've talked about so far – passion, balanced goals, planning – are so important. It's so much easier to say "no" to unimportant activities when you're in pursuit of goals about which you're passionate.

As you go through your daily and weekly activities, make time for yourself and for your family. Take off work and go on a school field trip with your child. Meet your spouse for lunch. Take vacations. Plan your family's investments. Fix up the house. Exercise. Eat right. Read.

The same holds true for your important business activities. Engage in reflection and proactive planning. Revisit your goals on a regular basis. Review the numbers. Meet with your team regularly. Go to conferences. Keep up with business trends and with your industry.

Build your business and live your life in a way that doesn't lead to regret later in life. It can be done. Thousands of others have done it. So have I, and you can, too.

It comes down to decisions. You make decisions every day about how to spend your time and how to manage your life. You're not a helpless bystander. You're in charge. Make the right decisions.

Get organized

To make good use of your time, you must be organized. You not only need to organize your schedule, you also need to organize your *stuff*. You must be able to find things when they're needed: Names, phone numbers, addresses, files, records, papers, keys, passwords, reference materials, facts, figures, bids and quotes, books, receipts. Anything that you need to find in the future – whether stored electronically or in hard-copy form – needs to be organized so you can lay your hands on it when needed.

If you're disorganized, people notice. Part of your "dependability quotient" is tied up in your level of organization (or disorganization.) Your subordinates, colleagues, customers and vendors must be able to rely on you to find documents and other items when needed, to show up on time, to safeguard items entrusted to you without losing them, and to at least come across as semi-organized. If not, your credibility will suffer.

And, if you're disorganized, you'll waste your time and the valuable time of others.

If you can't get organized on your own, seek help. There are many books on the subject, and in recent years an entire industry has emerged to help individuals and businesses in this area. A web search on the word "organizers" will turn up organizing consultants, speakers, trainers, and manufacturers of organizing products.

Get a calendar and ~~use it~~ live by it

Have you visited an office supply superstore lately? Most of them have an entire aisle dedicated to calendars, planners (I use the words calendar and planner interchangeably) and related accessories. There are dozens of formats available: hard-bound, spiral bound, three ring, large, small ... you name it. If you're so inclined, you can use an electronic calendar and avoid paper altogether.

You may already have a favorite format. If not, ask some friends and colleagues what they like. Get one, try it, and if it doesn't work for you then try another format next year.

Whichever way you go, though, you really need to have some sort of calendar/planner ... even if your business doesn't require lots of appointments. If nothing else, as you'll see shortly, I'm going to encourage you to schedule appointments with yourself. You read that right – with yourself.

While I'm in no position to tell you what format to use, I will offer these guidelines:

- If you're just getting started with a planner, use paper. Stay away from PDAs (Personal Digital Assistants) at first.
- Maintain just one calendar. Put all your personal and business activities and appointments in it.
- Make it portable so you can take it with you, rather than a wall or desk calendar.

Once you have it, use it. *Live by it.* Every single scheduled activity goes in it. Review it daily.

Schedule Your Personal Life

Here's why I'm so adamant about planners. If you already have a business, you know how hectic it can get. If you become a dedicated calendar user and something gets scheduled, there is a high likelihood it will get done. Not only does your calendar help you avoid the embarrassment of missed appointments, it is a way to ensure that you meet your obligations to yourself and your family ... to put focus where it's needed. If the only way to make sure you get to the school play is to get it in your planner, then get it in your planner. Schedule your exercise. Heck, schedule dinner at home if that's what it takes to get you there.

I've talked quite a bit about "balance" so far in this book, both directly and indirectly via references to family and personal life. I've talked about making "yes" and "no" decisions. *Turn your personal "yes" decisions into calendar entries, and then do them as scheduled.*

Schedule Your Business Life

The same concept holds true on the business side of the equation. Your planner is your ticket to continuous learning, important time with your staff, getting out to visit customers, and all the other important activities that go into the building of a successful business. *Turn your business "yes" decisions into calendar entries, and then do them as scheduled.*

Schedule Appointments with Yourself

Unless you have self-discipline well beyond that of most mortals, you'll need to schedule time for reflection, review, goal-setting and planning. If you leave it at "I'll just do it periodically", it probably won't happen.

How much time? And how often? Each person and each business has a rhythm. It might depend on how far ahead you plan, how fast your company is growing, and on your own personality.

Here is a sample of the kind of work I'm describing:

When?	How much time?	What to do?
End of the day	15 minutes	Review the day, enter notes from the day's work, and plan tomorrow
End of the week	30 minutes	Review the week and plan next week. Review selected key performance indicators.
End of the month	1 hour	Review the month including monthly and year-to-date financials, review business plans and projections for the new month, review goals.
End of the quarter	2 hours	Review the quarter including monthly, quarterly and year-to-date financials, review business plans and projections for the new quarter, review goals. Review personal finances and investments.
End of the year	Half a day	Review the year including all financials, review business plans and projections for the new year. Revisit your 3-5 year goals and vision. Think "big picture."

Of course, this isn't all the thought and planning that goes on. If you have a management team, you'll engage in business goal-setting and planning in meetings with them. The time scheduled with yourself is largely for reflecting on your personal goals and on what the business is doing – and should be doing – to keep you moving toward those goals.

Admittedly, the chart above seems heavily slanted toward business measures and issues. It is, and for good reason. Remember, your business is a tool whose purpose is serving you and your family. Scheduling time for reflection and review is one way to prevent the "business for the sake of business" trap we talked about earlier in the book.

"I make good use of time. I use a calendar, and I schedule personal time and planning time for myself." Can you honestly make this statement?

11. Values: The *Real* Boss

"We have a written list of values, everyone knows them, and they truly guide our actions."

Let's talk briefly about big businesses. Fortune 500 companies. The S&P 500. Publicly-traded companies. The big guys.

When you think of big companies, are you reminded of the good things they do? After all, big firms provide millions of jobs, they design and build the cars we drive, and provide many of our modern innovations. Many of these firms install on-site day care centers for their employees and donate large amounts of money to worthy causes. Many large companies are outstanding corporate citizens who inspire fervent loyalty among their employees, customers, and the communities in which they operate.

Or, when you think of big companies, are you reminded of mass layoffs, big-box chain stores running little guys out of business, corporate scandals, insider trading, an endless stream of acquisitions, and a single-minded focus on profit and stock price at any cost? Maybe the phrase "big business" reminds you of the millions of jobs that have been transferred overseas.

You'll probably agree that the general populous largely favors the latter outlook on big business. The very phrase "big business" has almost taken on a negative connotation. "Big Oil" certainly has.

Interestingly, though, people still love to own big company stocks and love to work for big companies.

Equally interesting is the fact that most big companies now have some version of a set of values or guiding principles that they've adopted.

It's not my aim to condemn or defend big business. But in a chapter on values in business, I think it's important to note that it's becoming increasingly difficult to see where values are playing a guiding role at large companies – notwithstanding the "Values Statements" hanging on their walls.

Small companies, happily, have not been painted with the same brush as big businesses. We continue to enjoy the respect and admiration of most Americans.

Let's keep it that way.

Regardless of your opinion of big business, and whether big business gets it right or wrong, small businesses – *your* business – can get it right. Doing the right thing and making a healthy profit are not mutually exclusive goals.

There's an old saying: "Nice guys finish last." I reject that notion. Instead, I prefer this one: "What goes around comes around." Do right or do wrong. Either way, you'll get your due.

An old-fashioned idea? Yep. Naive? Maybe.

In my mind, "values" is a hard-hitting, down-to-earth business issue – right along with revenues, net profit and return on assets. In a small, privately-held business, it's a particularly important subject because the company is a reflection of its owner.

If a business is looking for a bedrock foundation upon which to build, this is it. You can change the company's name, move to a new address, change employees, and even change the business model. But, if you have a solid set of values in place that the owner is passionate about (there's that word again), they offer a consistency and a continuity that survives all those changes. They provide guidance to employees – whether or not the owner is present. They attract and give assurance to customers, suppliers and lenders. They provide a stable base for business decisions of all kinds. Your values are on the job 24 hours a day, 7 days a week.

"Values" should be part of your strategy for success.

How are Values used in a practical, day-to-day business setting?

I could fill many dozens of pages in answer to this question. Instead, I'll offer a short list of examples:

- Your organization's values act as a "filter" through which you look when making any sort of people decisions: hiring, firing, rewarding, and promoting. We'll go into detail on this in chapters 12 and 13.
- They help you choose business associates, including customers and vendors. They also help you decide who to drop as an associate. Over the years, I've personally turned away business from prospective customers, and have "fired" both customers and vendors because of their values ... or lack thereof.
- Your values help you make decisions about business expenditures. For instance, if you claim "innovation" as a core value, you'd better be putting some money into R&D. If "employee safety" is important to your company, it would be tough to justify a dark factory full of outdated, unsafe machinery.
- The list could go on and on. A company interested in "civic duty" or "being a good corporate citizen" had better cooperate when employees get called for jury duty or National Guard duty. If "continuous learning" is one of your values, then support and encourage your people to seek educational opportunities, both on and off the job.

Some of you may be thinking, "That sounds like a lot of extra work. Who has time to go through all these extra steps?" Here is my response.

If you and your people truly believe in your values, these decisions are on auto-pilot. There are no "extra steps." Using values to guide your business isn't a "program." It's a way of doing business. You wouldn't have to think about whether it's OK to steal or leave the scene of an auto accident. You already have a built-in moral compass. Your company uses its values as *its* moral compass. The answer, more often than not, is obvious.

Sometimes, though, the answer to business problems is not obvious. If not, have a discussion about the situation. Weigh the pros and cons. Let all sides be heard. These types of discussions go a long way toward reinforcing the values you've adopted. Think of the message it sends to your people: Your organization believes in its values so strongly that it takes the time to stop and analyze a business decision *in the context of its values* before moving forward.

What about companies who don't claim to embrace any specific values?

All companies have values. Values are part of a company's culture; they are unavoidable. Whether or not the ownership intends it, values "happen."

There's an old saying: "If you choose not to decide, you still have made a choice." I think it applies here.

Wouldn't you prefer to take proactive measures to instill your values into your company, instead of watching from the sidelines and accepting whatever outcome happens on its own?

How do we choose our values and then embed them into the company?

Let me first tell you how they *don't* get chosen. They don't make your list because they sound good or because you think customers will like them.

I suggest a three-step process:

1. **Inject your own values but involve the entire company in the process.**
   From the very start, let your staff know what you're doing, why you're doing it, and solicit their input. Get your team involved in the exercise of choosing your company's values. Let them know why you're doing it: It's not a "program of the month." This is going to be part of the way the company does business. As with any other business initiative, folks will buy in much more readily if they play a part in the decision and implementation.

   In a way, you don't choose your company's values. You already have them. They are *your* values. Of course, everyone could name a long list of values that are important to him or her. But not all would be applicable to your business. And, even if they were, you wouldn't want a long list of values that reads like the phone book.

   If you are a start-up, reflect on your own personal values. If you're an established company, also think about the things the company does – the way the company acts – that make it what it is. What has made it successful? Why do customers keep coming back? What beliefs are already in place? What values do your best people bring to the organization?

Hold a brainstorming session free from interruptions. Have the participants throw out words and phrases. Someone writes them on a white board or a flip chart for all to see. Accept all answers. Once you start running out of responses, go back through and look for redundancies. Start weeding them out. You might get it down to a working list of 10-15 values, and schedule another meeting in a few days to further whittle it down after everyone has had time to think about it. Take as much time as needed to adopt a list of values that the owner strongly believes in and values by which the company will be guided. Try to limit your list to about six.

2. **Teach your values.**
   Make sure everyone knows them. Post them prominently. Talk about them frequently. Find examples of your values in action and discuss them. Create "teachable moments" that can be added to your base of company stories, to be told over and over again. Your company's stories are a great way to train new employees and to build teamwork, comradery, and employee loyalty.

3. **Live your values.**
   Make it clear that the company will never compromise its values, and then stand by that statement. Everyone in the company makes all decisions with your values in mind. Everyone practices what they preach – especially the management team.

This values stuff isn't easy. I guarantee you will run into situations that will challenge your resolve. You may have to let a key employee go, stop doing business with an important supplier, or pass up a significant revenue opportunity. There will almost without a doubt be times when a steadfast adherence to your values will cost you money ... short term. But the long-term payoff comes in many forms: The trust of all your stakeholders, more business from more customers as word gets around about how you do the right thing, your own sense of honor, and a self-policing culture.

In fact, this last one – a self-policing culture – is the surest sign that your company has truly embedded values into its culture. It's how you know when your values have become part of the "corporate DNA." Your people will talk about values without being prompted to do so. They'll take an active interest in who is being hired – about who is being allowed into their company. Mainly, *your people will hold each other accountable for values infractions.*

And each one of them will watch you like a hawk, to make sure you're setting the example.

Reaching this point won't happen overnight. It will take months – maybe years. But it is a critical component in having a life outside your business. At most firms, it's "when the cat's away, the mice will play." But not at your company. Once your values become the *real* boss, your people will do the right thing – they'll do it your way - and you won't have to be there to make it happen.

"We have a written list of values, everyone knows them, and they truly guide our actions." Can you honestly make this statement?

A real-life story from my first company:

My first company was a medical electronics sales and service business. Bloomington Hospital in Bloomington, Indiana sent us a $3500 item which we repaired and sent back via RPS. (Remember RPS? They were a small-package ground shipper in the 1990s. They were eventually acquired by FedEx and became FedEx Ground.) Anyway, the package got damaged on the way back to the customer. The local RPS claims rep took the package with him - although he wasn't supposed to – and lost it! We ran our claim all the way up to the VP level and even though RPS readily admitted they lost the equipment, they refused to pay for it. (Needless to say, this is one of the vendors we fired for not living up to our values. I was ashamed of RPS.) Not willing to leave our customer in the lurch, my company bought a new product for them. We hadn't done anything wrong, but we listed among our values both "Integrity" and "Customer Focus." $3500 was a *lot* more money to us than it would have been to RPS.

I admit that this is a (thankfully) rare and fairly extreme example of doing the right thing. I offer this story to point out how living your values can be painful and costly in the short term. "Putting your money where your mouth is" can take on a stinging reality.

12. Get the right people on your team ...

"We make sure to only hire the right people. If we don't know we've found the right candidate, we keep looking."

You can hire hard and manage easy, or vice versa. It's your choice.

Your hiring process is the single most important activity you'll engage in as a business person. Nothing else even comes close.

Get it right, and you'll make more money, enjoy being a business owner, and generally set yourself up for smooth sailing.

Get it wrong, and your life will be miserable.

I'm not exaggerating.

Let me share a lesson with you that I learned the hard way. In my early days as a business owner, I put about 75% of my hiring focus on work experience and education. The other 25% went into trying to decide things about personality, honesty and loyalty. In fact, it might have been more like 80/20, or even 90/10. The point is, I put way too much emphasis on so-called "job qualifications" and way too little on character and values.

After years of low morale, lower performance, high turnover, and all the chaos caused by these issues, I flipped the equation. I started putting *at least* 75% of my emphasis on character and values, and maybe 25% on training and experience. "Hire for attitude, train for skill" may not be right on the mark, but it's the only cliché that fits so we'll go with it. (My affinity for clichés should be well-established by now.)

Let's look at some ways to let the good ones in and keep the bad ones out. It shouldn't surprise you that it will involve values.

Your primary focus should be on finding employees who share your values. Note that I didn't say "finding employees to whom you can teach your values", or "finding employees into whom you can instill your values." You need to find folks who *already* share your values. You can't change people. Don't bother to try. If one of your company's stated values is "Respect for Others", and someone hasn't learned to treat others with respect by the time you find him, it's too late. Hey, his parents had him for twenty years. If they couldn't teach him respect, what makes you think you can?

Certainly, a job candidate needs certain qualifications. Education and experience count. I'm not suggesting you hire unqualified folks who happen to share your values. I am suggesting that you start with a pool of qualified candidates, and summarily reject any and all who don't measure up on the values scale.

Rule Number One: Avoid Being Sued

Find out what you can and cannot legally ask candidates. For instance, you can't ask questions intended to determine age, religion, marital status, or ethnic origin. Other questions are similarly off-limits. Do your homework.

Start with a Job Description

Each position in your company should have a job description. At minimum, it should consist of the job title, who the person reports to (preferably by title rather than by name), and a list of duties and responsibilities. Keep the list of duties general ... big picture in scope. Save the detail for a separate procedure for that duty. We'll get into creating procedures in Chapter 14.

The reasons for creating job descriptions include:
- It forces you to think through what a new addition to your company will be doing. (In fact, this thought process might cause you to re-think whether you even need to add to headcount.)
- It helps you set competitive compensation for that position.
- It helps you define the educational and experience requirements for the position.
- It helps you set performance standards for that position. (And, these standards can be written into the job description if you prefer.)

- Every employee deserves to know the answers to questions like: "Who is my boss?" and "What is expected of me?"

Each job description's list of duties should include "Other duties as assigned" to maintain flexibility.

Recruiting & getting the word out – Getting to the best candidates

Word of mouth might be a good approach. You might also consider using an outside agency like a temporary employment firm or recruiter who can pre-screen and pre-qualify your candidates. Then there are newspaper and internet ads. However you choose to get the word out to prospective employees, make your company's values part of the message. It will help turn away most (but not all) of the folks who don't share your values, and will attract many who do.

Screening Resumes

Since it's almost impossible to divine someone's values from an application or a resume, you'll do your initial sorting based on other criteria. Look for the obvious education, training and experience qualifications you've specified. Also look for things like bad grammar, poor spelling, and the quality of the cover letter if one is provided. (Even if the job doesn't require good grammar or spelling skills, major mistakes on the resume in these areas may be indicators of poor preparation and lack of attention to detail.) Sort resumes into three categories: Yes, no and maybe ... referring to whether their qualifications look like they rate an interview. After all are sorted, go back through them and see if you still agree with your initial assessment.

Conduct phone interviews to confirm each candidate's primary information on the resume, such as past jobs, education, and so on. Don't try to sell the candidate on your company at this point. If the candidate impresses you, schedule an in-person interview. If, at any time during the proceedings the candidate clearly isn't shaping up, don't waste any more of your time. Thank the candidate for his or her interest and end the conversation.

Interviewing

I recommend a multi-tiered approach to interviewing. By that I mean
multiple interviews (2 is OK; 3 is better) by multiple people in your
company. Consider panel interviews. The interviewing panel might
consist of you, the manager to whom the new hire will report, some or all
of the management team, and future peers of the prospective employee.

I also recommend a set of pre-determined questions – an interview form.
Asking the same questions of all candidates ensures consistency and
thoroughness. It also allows you to compare apples to apples. (There's
another of those pesky clichés.)

The interview should focus on open-ended, behavioral questions, and not
yes/no questions. Ask questions that get to the candidate's attitudes
toward your values, work ethic, customer service, getting along with
others, honesty, reliability and so on by finding out *how they did behave
in the past or would behave in the future.* Also, probe into their prior
jobs, going back no more than five years or so.

Be prepared to dig deeper and ask for more detail. Don't let the candidate
off the hook too easily and don't simply accept the first answer to a
question. Ask things like "What do you mean by that?" "Please expand
on that." "Why did you do that?" "What happened as a result?"

The reason you have to do this may surprise you: *Job candidates are not
always 100% open and honest about themselves.* (Translation: They lie.)

Are you shocked?

Wouldn't it be nice if they always told the truth, the whole truth and
nothing but the truth? Imagine ...

Prospective boss: "Tell me how you behave around customers."

Prospective employee: "I curse, throw things, and then curl up in the
fetal position."

Prospective boss: "Well, I'm sorry we can't use you. Thanks for coming
in."

Not only is undesirable behavior more subtle than this, candidate
interview responses are also more subtle and less direct than you'd like.

That's why it's vital to dig into responses until you're satisfied that you have the whole story.

Following are some sample questions.

General
- What did you like about the job?
- What did you dislike about the job?
- What were your supervisor's positive points?
- What were your supervisor's negative points?
- If I spoke with that supervisor, what would he or she say are your positive and negative points?

Stress management/anger
- How do you handle yourself under stress and pressure?
- Have you lost your cool in the past few months? Tell me about it.
- What's the most angry you have been in years? Tell me about it.

Integrity
- Have you ever had a situation at work where someone pressured you to act dishonestly? Tell me about it.
- If you encountered unethical behavior how would you handle it?

Get the idea? Ask an open-ended question and then shut up. Let the candidate speak. Throughout the interview process, the candidate should do 75% of the talking.

Take notes and after the interview, all members of the team who were present should compare their notes, thoughts, reactions and concerns while it is still fresh in their memories.

Personality Testing

I know some business owners who swear by pre-hire personality testing, and others who get along well without it. If you choose to include this as part of your process, be sure to apply it consistently and fairly. (See Rule Number One again as a reminder.) There are a number of tests intended to determine personality type. Some are self-administered, for some you use an outside testing firm, and you can even hire an industrial psychologist to do this for you. A quick search on the web or in your local Yellow Pages will turn up plenty of sources.

In my opinion, personality testing becomes less important as your interviewing process becomes more sophisticated. If multiple parties conduct a series of three interviews, you ask a carefully-chosen battery of open-ended, behavioral questions, and you require detailed answers to combat evasiveness and deception, you may find personality tests to be unnecessary. You'll have to decide if it's right for your company.

Skills testing

Depending on the nature of the position, this is a great way to find out who knows what. My first company was in electronics, and we used a written test for prospective repair technicians. It had 20 or so multiple-choice questions. Even though we chose fairly simple questions, you still had to know your stuff to do well on the test. This simple 15 minute exercise quickly pointed out the folks with a weak technical background.

You could do the same, and it doesn't have to be a written test. You could have a plumber solder pipes, have an electrician wire a socket, have a typist type ... just get creative.

Temporary employment agencies generally do a good job at this, especially for administrative personnel. Many firms hire via "temp-to-perm" so they can take advantage of these skills testing services.

Background checks and other pre-hire work

Get as much information from prior employers as possible. The #1 question to ask previous employers is: "Would you rehire this person?"

Pre-hire checks to consider include criminal history, driving record, drug screening, and a credit check. Again, do your homework and stay within legal limits.

In summary ... take your time. Skip parts of the process or rush at your own peril. You or members of your team will be tempted to do so. "We're so swamped. We need someone now. This first candidate seems OK. Let's cut the process short and get him on board. Next time we have an opening we can do it right." I urge you to not give in to this temptation. *Not* hiring is 1000% better than *bad* hiring.

"We make sure to only hire the right people. If we don't know we've found the right candidate, we keep looking." Can you honestly make this statement?

13. ... and keep them there.

"We retain our employees using competitive pay & benefits, and via our positive, high-involvement culture."

"Your people are your most valuable resource."

That phrase is so cliché and so over-used, even *I* have trouble using it. But it's true ... assuming you're hiring smart.

You invest time and money into hiring the right folks. You bring them into your company, teach them skills, and they get to know your customers and suppliers. Eventually, they get to be very good at what they do. When an employee leaves the business, it creates a void that must be filled. It's a major step backward. Think of the lost momentum, the lost expertise. Now, energy and time that might have been spent building on that momentum and expertise - moving forward and growing the company – must be wasted finding and training a replacement. It may be years before that department is back where it was.

High employee turnover is a business killer! A good goal: Keep turnover well below norms for your industry.

Before we start talking about how to keep your good people, let's talk about why and how to *not* keep non-producers, trouble-makers and other deadwood employees.

Out with the bad

If you have problem employees, I don't have to tell you about the negative affects they can have on your business and on you personally. Aside from the direct impact of a bad attitude or poor productivity, you can bet it also indirectly affects your operation in other ways. Primarily, it sends the wrong message to your good staff members and hurts their attitudes. Not only do they not want to be around the bad folks, they wonder why you leave someone like that on the team.

You basically have three options with poor performers:
1. Coach them to success
2. Reassign them to positions where they can contribute
3. Fire them

You may be thinking of a fourth option - tolerate them. Bad idea. It pulls the team morale down and hurts the company.

Having said this, getting fired should never be a surprise. Every employee should know how he or she is doing. When there's a problem, address it head-on. Clearly tell the employee what's wrong and what he or she needs to do about it. Document your conversations and when giving formal "shape up or ship out" warnings, do it in writing.

Now on to the fun stuff ... keeping good employees.

Pay and Benefits

We'll get into the work environment and how you treat your staff later, and that's important. But if you don't have a competitive basic compensation package you can't expect to attract and retain quality employees.

You can get average wage information by job title and company size from a variety of sources: the internet, trade associations, the government, etc. In my town, St. Louis, we have an organization called AAIM Management Association. They conduct annual wage and benefits surveys that can be purchased both by members and non-members. You probably have a similar organization in your city.

Whether or not you offer fringe benefits – and which ones you offer – depends on your industry and the companies you're competing against for employees. My personal philosophy is to be *competitive with pay and generous with benefits.* Here's why: I don't like customers who will switch to my competitor for a slightly cheaper price and similarly, I don't like employees who will jump ship for a small raise. I don't want to put the focus on price or salary. Let's be price or wage competitive but try to make something else the focal point. A good benefits package says, "I care about you and your family." It develops loyalty.

When designing your benefits package, don't overlook opportunities to save money – yours and the employees' - through the tax code. An IRS Section 125 "cafeteria" plan is easily implemented and administered. It saves payroll taxes for you and the employee, and lets the employee pay his or her portion of healthcare insurance via pre-tax dollars. The 529 college savings plans are becoming popular, and they let your employees put tax-advantaged money away for their kids' education.

Benefits and their tax implications is a subject where business owners would be well-advised to do some self-education. There are so many programs available that you don't want to be at the mercy of insurance salespersons for knowledge. I'm not suggesting you become a CPA or a know-it-all benefits expert. I am suggesting that you bone up on the basics of small business benefits Find out what similar sized firms are doing, and why.

Orientation Period

The first few months after someone joins your company are critical. Don't just throw someone into the mix and hope they find their way. Each new employee's supervisor should spend time training, getting the person's work area set up, introducing the new person to the other team members, and generally getting him or her off to a successful start. Other managers and coworkers can also help in this activity. Creating an orientation plan or checklist will ensure a consistent, thorough experience for all new hires.

Working Environment and Culture

You may want to create a company with employees who can't wait to get to work, smile all day, and who hate to leave at night. Good luck.

But if you want to create a company whose employees are involved and engaged, and are acting in the company's best interest ... it's very achievable. But, like virtually everything else discussed in this book, it requires effort and time.

In a nutshell: People want respect, feedback, appreciation, encouragement and praise. Give it to them.

What do I mean by "involved and engaged"? Perhaps I can best illustrate by showing you what it is not.

Suppose I droop into work – rarely on time. I go to my workstation and do as little as possible to get by. Anything short of a fire could happen around me and I will ignore it because it's not my job. The only time I move fast is at quitting time. I don't want to do anything to help my company's owner make more money because he already makes too much. Of course, I expect to receive a raise every year.

Folks, this is *not* a productive, involved or engaged employee.

When I talk about employee involvement, I'm talking about a situation where the company respects the employees' intelligence enough to want them for something more than turning a wrench. They also want their best ideas. By engagement I mean the employee is in tune with and is working toward the company's goals – it's a win-win relationship and everyone – employer and employee – are on the same page.

We all know that a terminally negative employee like the one I described is the exception. Most employees are not negative, but *are* less involved and less engaged than they could be. So let's talk about getting to *those* folks and getting them fired up about the company.

One approach is open book management. When I mention this to most of my fellow small company owners, they over-react. "Show my employees our revenue or profit? You must be kidding! If they see the numbers, they'll all want a raise! What if my competitors see the information?"

To the first point about your folks wanting a raise ... first of all, they want a raise *anyway*. And, they probably assume the company makes even more than it does. And so what if your competitors do see your numbers? What will they do differently? Realistically, these are not valid concerns.

Open book management doesn't necessarily mean showing everything. In fact, open book management is almost misnamed. What I'm really talking about is business literacy.

Let's say you have problems with attitude ... folks complain when new business comes in. "More work for us" they moan. Or, perhaps you have issues with waste of materials or money. Here's an exercise that any company can do to start moving down the right road:

Gather your employees together and tell them you're going to have a group discussion about why they should care about the company's financial success.

First, pull out a dollar bill and ask, "For each dollar of sales we take in, how much profit do you think the company gets to keep after paying our employees and all our other expenses?" You'll probably hear 30% ... 40% ... 50% ... as high as 60%, when the reality is that for most firms it is somewhere from 5% to 15%. This is a big eye-opener for most employees.

Then ask, "Who here wants to get a raise every year? Who expects the company to pay its share of the 20% health insurance premium increase we get each year?" Of course, everyone does. Then ask, "Where will the money to cover these additional expenses come from?" The answer, obviously, is that the company must continue to bring in additional revenue to cover these growing expenses. *Now* the light bulbs start to come on.

Can you see that we're practicing open book management – more accurately, we're teaching business literacy – without showing a single number? Now, this is not a one-meeting, one-discussion subject. It's a long, drawn-out process that takes dedication. But if you stick with it, show some actual numbers, set goals, and even go so far as to attach potential bonuses to the company's financial results – little by little over time, your employees will see you're serious about acting in their best interests, and they will begin to see the wisdom in acting in the company's best interest.

The best companies – big and small – are the ones who have taken the time to get their employees engaged in the company's goals and involved in the pursuit of its success.

If you take the time and invest the effort to create this type of culture in your company, your employees will go beyond simply performing their jobs.

Performance Management

Most managers and business owners like performance appraisals about as much as a sharp stick in the eye. They dread them. They postpone them. They avoid them and hope the employees don't ask about them.

If your concept of "performance management" revolves around a formal, sit-down, once-a-year meeting where a manager surprises a subordinate with a laundry list of things he or she doesn't do right, I encourage you to start thinking differently about it.

Performance management is not an annual event. It's an ongoing process.

Think of a coach, working to get the best performance out of a team. What sort of results could be expected if the coach only met with the team members at the end of the season to review statistics and performances?

Of course you want your employees to be satisfied, motivated, energized and doing a high volume of their best work. Then you've got to let them know how they're doing.

It involves frequent feedback – both positive and constructive criticism. Encouragement. Private and public praise. Recommendations for improvement. Telling and showing. Thanks. Congratulations.

This feedback should cover all the bases. Don't just focus on job output or quantity. Look at quality. Look at dependability. And, be sure to focus on values: Does the employee live and model the company's values? I'm repeating myself because it's an important point: *All people decisions – hiring, firing, rewarding and promoting – should be made largely on the basis of values.*

No matter what you call it ... coaching, performance management, feedback, insert-your-own-word-here ... it is absolutely essential if you have employees.

Having said all this, I also believe that some sort of written, documented formal process has a role to play. But:
- The manager's comments should never be a surprise to the employee. If the manager is doing a good job, the employee already knows

exactly what the manager thinks of his or her performance, and the formal review is just documentation.

- The formal review is no substitute for regular, ongoing daily and weekly feedback.
- The purpose of a formal appraisal is not just to determine a pay raise. Don't condition your employees to directly link the timing of reviews with the implementation of raises. Both the manager and the employee should look forward to reviews for the sake of the employee's performance and contributions to the company ... not because of the impact on pay.

There is no "one size fits all" approach to formal performance appraisals. Annually seems to be a good cycle for most organizations. Following are two methods for you to consider:

- **Use job descriptions.** Simply use the employee's job description and go through each duty or responsibility. While most companies use the traditional "1 through 5" rating, I prefer verbiage. Write out your comments under each duty. How is the employee doing? What is being done well? How could it be done better? Give specific examples.
- **Use a paragraph style.** The first section might be your comments on all the positives – things the employee does well, areas where improvement has been noted, good suggestions, and so on. The next section would focus on opportunities for improvement – things the employee could do better, suggestions for training, and weaknesses that could be shored up. Finally, summarize the employee's performance and end on a high note.

Two final recommendations about performance reviews:

- Strive for a balance between positive and negative feedback. Encourage and congratulate more than you criticize. When you have to criticize, do so constructively. (By the way, I believe you can be tough and firm and still be supportive. I'm not suggesting you walk on eggshells here. Just remember these are people you want on your side, acting in the company's best interests. "Respect" and "Professionalism" are two good words to keep in mind.)
- Forward planning should be a big part of the process. Don't just look at what the employee did this past year. What will be done in the future? What training is planned? Is he or she interested in and qualified for more responsibility?

Employee satisfaction surveys

Periodic written surveys to find out what your employees are thinking are a good idea. I suggest once per year. Don't assume they're happy ... ask them. Have employees respond anonymously so they feel free and safe to share their real thoughts. Ask them for feedback on pay, benefits, training, advancement opportunities, company culture, company leadership and more.

"We retain our employees using competitive pay & benefits, and via our positive, high-involvement culture." Can you honestly make this statement?

14. Policies, Procedures, and Systems

"We use written Policies, Procedures, & Systems to ensure quality, consistency & to minimize reinventing the wheel."

Successful companies don't make it up as they go along. For your company to be successful, you need a set of policies, procedures and systems. The larger and more complex your company, the more numerous and sophisticated your needs in this area.

Policies

Whether written or not, every company has policies. Policies cover things like whether a product can be returned, under what circumstances an employee will be fired, how long an employee needs to be on the job before being eligible for health insurance, what constitutes sexual harassment, and whether company computers may be used for personal emails.

Keep your policies simple, clear, consistent with your values and *as few as possible*. Don't create a policy for everything, but do create them for important issues.

Don't hide behind "It's our policy." Be willing to bend when appropriate. Do what's right – not just what the policy says to do.

A good time to develop a policy is when someone asks for the first time, "What is our policy for ...?" If it's an important issue, you don't have an answer and you expect the question to come up again in the future, you may as well go ahead and develop a policy to cover that situation. Discuss among the management team or, if appropriate, get an attorney involved.

Procedures and Systems

Can you imagine a fast food restaurant that allowed each employee to
decide how to make a burger? Or a bank without formal processes for
accepting a deposit?

I'm not suggesting creation of unnecessary red tape, bureaucracy, or
nonsense.

- I am suggesting that once someone spends the time to figure out how
  to do something, it's a waste to let other employees spend the time
  (also known as "money") to figure it out again.
- I am suggesting that it is irresponsible to let the company's know-how
  go out the door daily at 5PM.
- I am suggesting that you don't want important business processes to
  be done "Jim's way" or "Judy's way" or "Jethro's way." You want
  important business processes done *the company's way!*
- I am suggesting that the *only* path to consistent product and service
  quality is to have procedures and systems. They should be simple
  and clear.
- I am suggesting that when a new hire comes on board, you should be
  able to slide some papers across the table and say, "Go do this job."
  (I hope you wouldn't really do this but you should strive for having
  enough clearly written procedures so that you *could* do it.)

So, what's the difference between a procedure and a system? I can
probably best explain by example.

In a previous chapter we discussed hiring. You might have a procedure
for conducting a phone interview. (I use the word "procedure" pretty
loosely. It might just be a simple checklist. In my mind, a procedure is
anything in writing – even in pictures – to guide the steps someone takes
to accomplish a task.) Let's say you also have a checklist/procedure for
an in-person interview. You also have a job application and a form
asking for the applicant's approval to perform various background
checks.

All of these checklists, procedures and forms make up a hiring *system*.

Please don't get hung up on these terms. Feel free to give these things
different names. The important concept is documenting what you do,

who does it, when it gets done, and how it gets done in sufficient detail to ensure quality and consistency, and prevent duplication of effort.

Let's look at another example that can help make my point. Suppose you start a retail store and are the only employee. In the early days, you'll be doing all kinds of stuff ... some simple, some complicated, some repetitious, and some things you'll never have to do again. One task might involve buying and restocking product for sale in your store.

Suppose the steps you end up with are:

1. Determine which product needs to be ordered
2. Create purchase order
3. Fax purchase order to vendor
4. When order arrives, check received items against purchase order for accuracy
5. Mark purchase order "Received" and staple to vendor's shipping document
6. Place product in showroom display

Let's say you hire a new store sales employee, Kathy, and you want her to take over the purchasing process. Your training choices include:

- Show her how you do it, and hope she takes notes or has a good memory, or
- Type up the simple 6 step procedure shown above and give it to her while she's being trained.

Which do you think will work out best?

If you go the route of most small businesses – which is to show rather than write a procedure – eventually Kathy "gets it." She starts doing the job, becomes good at it, and over time probably adopts new approaches to the job that you don't even know about. These changes may be subtle or they may be very significant. They may be made for internal or external reasons.

Let's revisit our 6 step purchasing process. After a few months on the job, Kathy makes some discoveries and modifies the procedure. (Remember, none of this is written down. It's all in Kathy's head. There never was and still isn't any sort of documented procedure.)

- She finds out that of the company's 6 main suppliers, 2 strongly prefer to receive purchase orders via email. These two suppliers ship orders at least 24 hours sooner if the purchase order is emailed rather than faxed.
- She learns how to combine orders a certain way with each vendor to get better prices and avoid minimum order fees.
- She also knows that several of your vendors email order acknowledgements, which include the shipping carrier's tracking number and estimated delivery date. She gets in the habit of printing and stapling this document to the purchase order, and it has allowed her numerous times to help make a sale by telling the customer when an out of stock item will arrive.

After a year on the job, Kathy quits. All of this knowledge that Kathy gained – *which belongs to you* – walks out the door.

So you hire her replacement and show him how to do it the old way. You haven't been involved in purchasing for over a year. Kathy handled it. You don't know anything about all the discoveries she made or the changes she made to the process. You've lost a year's worth of important business knowledge ... because nobody bothered to write down a few simple bits of information.

By the way, if I didn't convince you in chapter 13 to avoid employee turnover, hopefully you're convinced now.

So, even if you're the only employee, take the time to write down what you do and how you do it. When you have time, put it in your computer and print it out. By the time you have your first employee, you will have a good start on an operation manual. Think how much easier it will be to train your folks and how much smoother the operation will run.

Even if you've already been in business for years and don't have written procedures, it's not too late. Get your employees involved. Have them write procedures for important processes. Nothing fancy is needed ... simply document the steps they go through.

But the longer you've been doing something, the greater the chance that you or your staff have fallen into the "we've always done it this way" trap. If you're finally putting these things in writing after months or years, take a little extra time to also *analyze how the activity is being done*. It's very likely that you'll find improvement opportunities, especially if you and your staff look at each others' work processes. An impartial outsider can often see things you can't because you're so close to the process. Coworkers are not exactly "impartial outsiders" but getting someone outside the process to evaluate it will almost certainly yield good discussion and suggestions. Warning: Some employees will have their egos bruised when others challenge their work. Remind everyone that the goal is improved efficiency ... not territorial protection. Stay involved. Publicly celebrate when improvements are discovered. Be sure to congratulate (and possibly even reward) all parties involved not only for the new-found efficiency, but also for cooperating. Rather than letting someone sulk because "they invaded my turf", make that person a hero. Done right, this sort of "re-engineering" exercise can have a major positive impact on your company's culture. It's a form of Continuous Improvement, which we'll cover in Chapter 20.

Successful companies - *like yours* - don't make it up as they go along.

"We use written Policies, Procedures, & Systems to ensure quality, consistency & to minimize reinventing the wheel." Can you honestly make this statement?

Keeping procedures and other documents updated ...

This applies to your policies, procedures, forms, job descriptions, sales literature and even your stationery. Include a revision date somewhere on the document. I like to put it at the very bottom in small print. Here's why: Over time, you or someone on your staff will update and modify your procedures, forms, and other materials. Without a revision date, how will you know which ones to keep and which ones to discard? How will you know if you're using the current one or an old version? This idea is easy to implement and simple to interpret. It saves time and prevents mistakes.

15. Wouldn't it be great if mistakes corrected themselves and never happened again?

"We use a corrective action system to identify & fix the root cause of errors and to prevent future problems."

All companies make mistakes. Every single company. Big. Small. Start-ups. One hundred year old firms. This is one thing your small business has in common with literally every company on the face of the Earth. We all screw up from time to time.

Errors come in all shapes and sizes. It may be accounting errors, billing errors, product quality mishaps, poorly executed customer service, late deliveries, shipments to the wrong addresses ... I can't list all the possible types of mistakes businesses make.

Mistakes are costly. They waste time, money, productivity and resources. They aggravate employees. They lose customers.

The difference between companies is not *whether* they make mistakes. The difference lies in what a company does about it *when* it makes a mistake.

Some companies blame anyone or anything other than themselves. If the error directly affected a customer, they might correct the outcome but rarely if ever acknowledge the mistake and rarely apologize. They act like you're imposing when you ask to have the mistake corrected and think they're doing you a favor when they correct their own mistake. And, this same mistake will be repeated over and over again. The company motto may as well be, "We never have time to do it right, but we always have time to do it over."

Ever get your order wrong at a fast food drive-up window? Then you know exactly what I'm talking about. (Perhaps a better question would be: Have you ever gotten your order *right* at a fast food drive-up window? Has *anyone ever* received a correct order from a fast food drive-up window?)

Other companies immediately spring into action and fall all over themselves to correct mistakes – especially for customers. They apologize. Depending on circumstances, they might offer the customer something extra to soften the impact of the error and to show the customer they're serious.

Clearly, the second type of company is where you want to be. Many companies, and I'd like to think most companies, are in this category. Most businesses do a pretty good job of making things right with the customer. And so should you.
But, I'm going to ask you to kick it up a notch. It's great to admit a mistake and get it corrected quickly, but what about the root cause of the mistake? Why did it happen? What can be done to prevent this same type of error from happening in the future?

Here's a simple example:

You own a florist business. You offer both red and yellow roses. A customer calls to order a dozen yellow roses for delivery and your company mistakenly sends red ones. Of course, you immediately send someone to deliver the yellow roses and apologize to the customer. After the fact, though, you investigate to find out what went wrong. You could simply talk to the person who took the phone order. (In fact, that's what most managers would do. They'd chastise the person and insist on accuracy in the future.) But you decide to look deeper, because this is not the first time this has happened – and it happens no matter who is on duty. You find out that your phone order form has no check boxes for color. It depends on the sales clerk to hand-write the color on the form. The form is redesigned with "Red" and "Yellow" check boxes. Over the next few months, no roses of the wrong color are sent out.

This is "root cause" thinking. In order for you to create the kind of "self-healing" company I'm describing here, you and all your people will need to get good at looking for the root causes of problems.

This is "company culture" stuff. Getting to the point where this approach to problem-solving is routine and comfortable takes hard work and lots of time. But, if you want your business to thrive, and if you want a life outside your business, it's vital.

It's not about the individual employee. It's not about blame. When errors occur, the person involved needs to admit it without fear of reprisal. If a customer or vendor is affected and brings it to your company's attention, the employee who receives the complaint should apologize on behalf of the company – whether or not he or she was responsible.

Drive individual blame and cover-ups out of your company. Replace them with openness and willingness to admit mistakes. It's about finding the root cause of errors and preventing them in the future. It's about learning from mistakes.

Now, if an individual employee has a genuine problem with accuracy or quality it clearly needs to be addressed. If he can't or won't improve, he probably has to go away. But don't jump to the conclusion that errors are necessarily the result of carelessness. Think root cause. Are the systems and support processes in place to ensure success? Has the employee received the right training?

Let's talk about formalizing this search for root causes of problems into a system ... a Corrective Action System. (Sounds bureaucratic, doesn't it?)

Why would a small to mid-sized company want to burden itself with extra paperwork in this way? Two reasons come to mind:
- Think of all the types of mistakes that can happen in your company, and the costs associated with letting the same mistakes happen over and over. If you could put a simple system in place that would stop mistakes in their tracks, why would you *not* use it?
- A written system moves the idea of root cause thinking from the abstract to real life. It becomes part of the job for everyone in the company.

Plus, if you plan to become ISO-9000 registered you will need a formal corrective action system anyway. Here's how it works ...

The formal Corrective Action System

Corrective Action Report

Opened by: _____ Date: _____

Brief description of the error:

How it was discovered or who reported it:

Did this incident directly affect a customer? [ ]Yes [ ]No

If so, which one: _____

Actions taken to satisfy customer:

By: _____ Date: _____

This issue was: [ ]Preventable [ ]Unpreventable

If preventable, the root cause was:
[ ]Human error by: _____
[ ]Other:

Action taken to prevent future recurrences:

Reviewed by: _____ Date: _____

First, someone has to coordinate this system. If the company is very small, it should probably be the company owner. If the business has 15 or more employees, this job can be delegated to any employee who can be trusted to impartially analyze problems without turning it into The Inquisition. We'll call this person – whomever it is - the coordinator. By the way, doing this work should not take more than an hour each week.

A flowchart is shown in Figure 15-1. Read the sequence below and then refer to the flowchart to see that it's simpler than it may sound the first time you read about it.

The process begins when someone inside or outside the company reports an error. If a customer is involved, the first and main goal is customer satisfaction! Someone – *anyone* – needs to take immediate action and make the customer happy.

After the immediate customer issue is resolved, the employee who first becomes aware of the problem opens a Corrective Action Report, or CAR. (But you can call it whatever you want to.) At least once a week, the coordinator reviews all open CARs, looking for new ones and also to keep all of them moving toward being resolved and closed.

The coordinator makes a judgment about each incident. Was it avoidable? If not, there's no more work to do on it. (No sense digging into unavoidable problems, right?) In this case, the CAR is closed and filed away.

If it appeared, though, to be an avoidable mistake, he or she analyzes what happened and who was involved. The overriding goal is to determine the root cause of the error. Ask questions and look at processes (or lack thereof.)

It may be determined that this was a simple human error. It happens. Folks make mistakes. In this case, you mark the form accordingly – including the person who made the error – close the CAR, and file it away. This should be done in a matter-of-fact way, without pouncing on the person who erred and without making it into a public affair. You want people to feel comfortable and safe reporting and admitting their own mistakes. The only way to reach that point is to make the environment and the process as benign as possible.

If the mistake was preventable and a root cause can be determined, *do something about it.* Change the process. Add a step. Do some training. Engage in some sort of proactive activity to prevent that same type of error from wasting time, money and customer goodwill in the future.

When you solve a problem using this approach, let everyone in the company know. Announce it and celebrate it. Let everyone know who came up with the fix, and let that person take the credit. Make a big deal of the fact that you have eliminated a potential future problem. This positive reaction helps validate your approach toward eliminating errors. But perhaps more importantly, it shines attention on the problem you just fixed ... further ensuring that it will stay front-of-mind with your people in the future.

So, now that I've described the system, let me go back and make some clarifications.

What sort of errors and mistakes should be targeted by the corrective action system? The answer is up to you. I suggest that you include at least these three:
- An order is shipped to the wrong address
- An order is filled incorrectly or incompletely
- A customer complaint is received

How serious should the error be to bother opening a CAR? Again, it's up to you, but remember that this process takes time, and time is money. Reserve the formal system for issues that seem the most likely to waste significant time, money, resources, or that seem likely to damage relationships with customers, vendors and other important business partners.

This may be the most important idea to take away from this chapter: *Attack the root causes of errors without placing individual blame.*

The same exact approach that is used in a formal written CAR can be applied to minor errors without writing anything down. Even for major issues, you may want a less formal yet written process. Perhaps when an error is caught, the person involved simply documents the situation in an email and sends it to the company president. *No matter how you handle the mechanics, get your people to adopt root-cause thinking and your error rate will shrink.*

Let's talk about this idea of "not placing individual blame." I've repeatedly made the point that blame has no place in this process. But I also have a place on the CAR for the name of the person who made a human error. Is this a contradiction? I don't think so.

As pointed out earlier, we all make mistakes. But we have to learn from our mistakes. If I goof up and it's pointed out to me, it's my responsibility to take steps to prevent that mistake in the future. I may need to slow down, be more careful, double-check myself, or seek training. But if I continue to make the same errors, I can't reasonably expect to stay in the same job. Good employees understand this, and

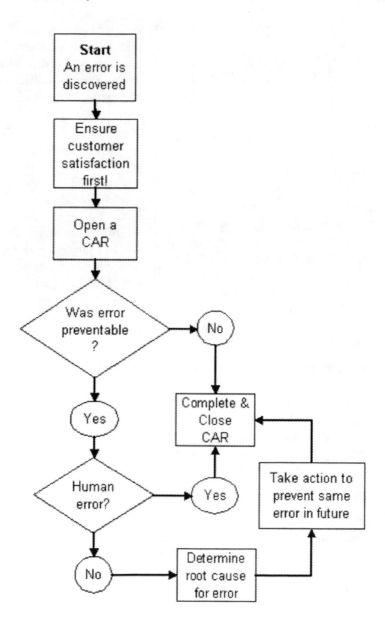

Figure 15-1
The Corrective Action System Flowchart

Corrective Action System ←
Paper or Electronic?

You can do this with paper, but I can tell you from personal experience that an electronic system (on a server, a web site, or an intranet site) is the way to go. Not only is it easier to use, it is infinitely better from an information retrieval standpoint. After all, you'll want to go back and look at your results. Do yourself a favor and keep paper out of the equation. I'm not going to go into detail here on the technical aspects of an electronic corrective action system, but think "database."

---

your company's morale will suffer if you allow anyone to continually produce shoddy work. There's a difference between knee-jerk blame and professionally dealing with a poor performer. Treat folks with dignity and respect but also insist on accuracy and quality. The two are not mutually exclusive.

All of the employees have to buy in to the idea that we're trying to drive repeat errors out of the company. We're not "writing someone up."

If Dave initiates a corrective action report because George put his right foot in when the Hokey Pokey song at the company barbeque said "put your left foot in", Dave has not fully embraced the spirit of the corrective action system.

If George initiates a corrective action report that involves Dave only because Dave had done so to George last week, George has not fully embraced the spirit of the corrective action system.

If you have employees like Dave and George above, go back and re-read chapter 12, where we discussed hiring the right people. While you're at it, re-read the section in chapter 13 titled "Out with the bad", where we discussed how and why to get rid of bad employees.

I offer the Dave and George scenario only partly tongue in cheek. *This system requires a high level of maturity by all involved.* Those initiating a CAR must be doing so for the right reason. Employees answering questions about errors must be open, honest and not inclined to "cover up" for someone. Pettiness, nit-picking, and immaturity are all at odds with the success of this system.

The chapter title asks the following question: Wouldn't it be great if mistakes corrected themselves and never happened again?

I'll answer my own question. Yes, it would be great. The bad news: It'll never happen. But here's the good news: You can come pretty close.

Make it the job of everyone in your company to identify and attack the root causes of errors.

"We use a corrective action system to identify & fix the root cause of errors and to prevent future problems." Can you honestly make this statement?

The task of identifying and fixing the root cause of an error doesn't necessarily fall on the company president, the coordinator, or on any single person. Sometimes, a group brainstorming session may be just the ticket.

At my first company, some of the best solutions to big problems came out of group meetings. Our service department would sometimes "farm out" work to the original equipment manufacturer. This caused all sorts of issues with lead times (due to the item being shipped out and back) and logistics in general. It made it virtually impossible to predict when the customer would get the item back or what it would cost. It frequently gave us a black eye with our customers and caused headaches for both our service and shipping departments.

I had personally tried to address this problem but nothing I came up with made it much better. I was unable to determine the real root cause for the problem. So, we convened a problem-solving meeting with the 8 or 9 people who were directly involved with the farm-out process. We spent two hours playing "what if" ... throwing out ideas and kicking them around. The result was some out-of-the-box thinking: The root cause of our problems wasn't *how* we handled farm-outs. *The problem was that we were handling them at all.* We had been subtly encouraging customers to send us items that we could not fix in-house. We completely shifted our thinking and started actively discouraging customers from sending us items that we could not repair in-house. This was completely contrary to our normal approach, which was to always say "Yes" to our customers. This proved to be exactly the right solution, and it didn't come from me. It came from rank and file employees.

You don't have all the answers. No one individual does. Tap into your company's collective brain-power.

16. Delegate or spin your wheels – it's your choice

"I delegate authority & allow others the freedom to determine how to reach the desired results."

> *"The greatest leader isn't necessarily the one who does the greatest things. The greatest leader is the one who gets the people to do the greatest things."*
> - Ronald Reagan

In chapter 12, I made this statement about hiring the right people: Get it wrong, and your life will be miserable.

It was a strong statement, and I meant it.

Here is an equally strong statement about delegation: If you don't delegate, your business will never realize its potential and you won't have a life outside your company.

Having the right people and then delegating to them ... these are the "one-two punch" of business success and having a life.

Why delegate?

Simply put, you can't do it all, so don't even try.

Remember the work we did in the early part of this book. Your business is a tool to enhance your life and the lives of your family. Your business exists to serve you, not the other way around.

If you don't delegate, you will quickly become a servant to the business. You'll become embroiled in every aspect of the company. The demands on your time will exceed your availability and will tax your patience.

I fell into this trap early in my career as an entrepreneur. Before I learned to delegate, I was the single biggest obstacle to my company's success. I should have been thinking about strategy and focusing on the big picture. Instead I was doing simple tasks better handled by others. In the words of my favorite motivational speaker, Jim Rohn, I was "majoring in minor things."

When you delegate:
- You show trust in others. This is good for morale.
- You develop others' skills. This is good for the business.
- You free up your time so you can do "CEO stuff" and have a life. This is good for the business *and* good for you.

What do I mean by "CEO stuff"? All the stuff in this book! Goal setting, planning, and executing. And the message of this chapter is: don't try to do it all yourself ... especially the execution. You're there to oversee, guide, train, educate, motivate, inspire and lead.

Of course, when you're getting started and have no staff, there's nobody to delegate to. Even then, creating policies, procedures and systems is laying the groundwork for the delegation you'll eventually do when you hire employees. It's never too early to either delegate or to prepare to do so.

You may be one of those business owners who believes "nobody can do it as well as I can." You may be right. But the key to business success does not lie in you doing everything. In fact, "you doing everything" stands smack dab in the way of business success. We're right back to hiring the right people. Put the right folks on your team, train them and trust them. Maybe they won't do it as well as you. Then again, maybe they'll surprise you.

Here's some food for thought about "nobody can do it as well as I can." Let's say you can do something extremely well. We'll call it 100% well. Each time you do it, it brings in a certain amount of money. Others can be taught to do it, but they only are at 90% of your competency level and only bring in 90% of the money you bring in. You can do it yourself once, bring in 100% of the money, and have your time monopolized. Or, you can multiply your effectiveness and have several (or even dozens) of others doing it while you oversee the operation and enjoy the results. Two people at 90% each equals 180%. Five people at 90% each equals 450%.

It's an abstract example but you get the point. In this example, not a single person to whom you delegate is as good as you. Why would you care?

One other argument that some small-company CEOs make goes something like this: "I'm not too good to do the work around here. I don't want my people to think I'm acting like a big-shot. I feel that I should be rolling up my sleeves and working right alongside my staff."

Delegating is not about being a big-shot or lording over people. Everyone in every organization has a job. If you're the CEO, your job is providing direction and strategy for the company. The smaller the company, the more hats you and everyone else must wear. But as you grow – in fact, if you *want* to grow – get used to wearing fewer "doing" hats and more "thinking" hats.

When and what to delegate

Jack Stack, one of the founders of Springfield Remanufacturing Corporation, author of the best-selling book *The Great Game of Business*, and the father of Open-Book Management says, and I paraphrase, *"If a CEO makes a decision that impacts the company inside of 30 days, it's a waste of the CEO's time. CEOs should delegate such short-term decisions to others, and spend time on long-term, big-picture strategy."* (By the way, if you haven't heard of Jack Stack, SRC, or the Great Game of Business, you're either brand new to the business world or have been in solitary confinement for the last twenty years. Either way, welcome. We discussed Open Book Management in chapter 13 and will get into it again in chapters 18, 19 and 20.)

For very small companies, you can't take Jack's advice literally. Small-business CEOs must be involved in some day to day activities. You simply don't have a large enough staff to allow you to spend all your time planning. And, a very small company doesn't warrant that much big-picture thinking. In fact, you may be the only employee. But the *spirit* of his statement could be applied to your company, regardless of its size. How about this:

**Before you start -or continue – to perform a task, ask yourself,
"Is this the best use of my time and talents?"**

and

**Continually ask yourself,
"Am I spending so much time *doing*
that I'm not spending enough time
goal-setting, planning, strategizing, leading, learning, and training?"**

Since each business is unique, it's impossible for me to offer a list of specific activities that you should or should not delegate. But look at any business from an outside, objective viewpoint and it becomes obvious which jobs are best done by rank-and-file, management, and senior leadership staff. Rank-and-file puts the ladder against the wall and climbs it, management makes sure it is being placed and climbed efficiently, and senior leadership makes sure it is leaning against the right wall. Look at your business from an objective viewpoint, and ask others to take a look as well. Make sure the appropriate people are doing the tasks that seem obvious to an outsider.

As you start hiring employees, begin thinking about developing a management team. Your management team consists of you and the employees you select to help you ensure business success. This is not "president by committee." You're still the CEO. Putting a management team in place is a way to delegate certain managerial duties to others. Each member is given responsibility for a certain part of the business along with the necessary authority. In small companies, there's a good chance that each management team member also has a "doing" job. For instance, the person who manages the accounting department may also handle accounts payable or billing. The sales manager may do some or all of the selling. In a small company, being on the management team doesn't necessarily mean you just manage.

The management team runs the various departments so the CEO doesn't have to be involved in and on top of every detail in every part of the company. Members communicate with each and meet regularly so everyone knows what's going on. Company-wide matters can be discussed and decisions rendered on a team basis. The CEO always has the final say, of course, but should always listen and take team members' input seriously. Once a decision is made, each member of the management team needs to support that decision fervently, even if he or she was initially against the idea. More on management team meetings in the next chapter.

In his classic book *The E-Myth*, small business guru Michael Gerber advises, "Work *on* your business, not just *in* your business." I could stay up all night and not think of a way to say it any better. (Gerber also inspired the title of this section of the book – the idea of creating a job, rather than a business.)

So, the question of "what and when to delegate" is peculiar to each company. The answer lies in this advice:

Look for situations and tasks that can and should be handled by others. Make the best use of your time and talents. Work *on* your business and not just *in* your business. Develop a management team and use the team to help with planning, execution, and to take on some or all of the supervisory workload.

How to delegate

Suppose you are overseeing a group of people about to assemble a jigsaw puzzle. You have several ways to approach this task. You could ...

1. hide the picture of the finished puzzle, then stand over their shoulders and direct them on the assembly piece by piece.
2. show them the picture of the finished puzzle and still direct them on the assembly piece by piece.
3. show them the picture of the finished puzzle and check on progress periodically
4. show them the picture of the finished puzzle and make yourself available for assistance if needed.
5. show them the picture of the finished puzzle and ask them to contact you only after the work is done.

*   Option 1 goes well beyond micro-managing and all the way to being a complete waste of your time. I can't think of a good reason to give a job to employees without letting them know what outcome is expected.
*   Option 2 can be either micro-managing (bad) or training (good.)
*   Options 3 through 5 are forms of delegation. Various facts will help determine how much follow-up and supervision is needed, such as the skill level of the people involved and how critical the job may be.

Here's a guideline for your consideration, assuming that the people doing the task are up to the job:

Let people know what outcome is expected and then get the heck out of their way. Make yourself available but make yourself scarce. Delegate results – not methods.

When you delegate to others, you're delegating authority but not the ultimate responsibility for the outcome. That stays with the leader. Sure, you give folks responsibility for a job and even for an entire department, and you hold them accountable. But you still must stay in contact and make sure they are on track. Your employees may shirk their responsibility, but if you're following up you'll know about it before things get too far off course. So, whenever you delegate to someone, keep a record of it and set up a reasonable reporting/follow-up schedule, something like this:

- Task delegated:
- Person to whom this task was delegated:
- Expected outcome:
- Timeframe for completion:
- Progress reports/follow-ups on these dates:

Both you and the person to whom you've delegated need to agree to the schedule and to the desired outcome. You might include a list of resources needed, and you also might make note of the expected amount of progress at each of your follow-up dates.

If you don't delegate, your business will never realize its potential and you won't have a life outside your company.

"I delegate authority & allow others the freedom to determine how to reach the desired results." Can you honestly make this statement?

17. We've got to start meeting like this

"Our meetings have an agenda; we stay on topic; decisions are documented including who will do what by when."

I decided to devote an entire chapter to the subject of meetings for a couple of reasons.

First, meetings that are unnecessary, poorly planned, or poorly run waste time like crazy. Multiply the participants' compensation times the number of hours the meeting lasts, and then factor in the opportunity cost (the productive things that might have been accomplished in the absence of a meeting) ... well, it adds up quickly.

Second, meetings are used to accomplish virtually everything I talk about in this book. Meeting with your spouse to do personal planning. Strategic planning meetings with your staff. Hiring. Delegating. Not much work in business goes on in a vacuum.

Planned or impromptu, formal or casual, love 'em or hate 'em ... meetings are a key part of business.

I have a neutral attitude about business meetings. I neither love nor hate them. To me, meetings are a natural, matter-of-fact and important component of business success. They're a form of communication, but they're also a unique way to get disagreements out in the open and then resolve them. And, they are a unique way to draw out good ideas that might have otherwise remained forever hidden. There is no substitute for good old eyeball to eyeball discussion.

In this chapter, we'll discuss the types of meetings for you to consider for your business. Then, I'll give you a formula for running a meeting for top efficiency and results.

Routine Management Team Meetings

You should meet with your management team on a regular basis –
probably weekly but some other frequency may work best for your
situation. I strongly recommend that you set aside the same day and time,
and then stick to it like glue. If you leave it to chance or don't have a
routine, I assure you that your meetings will be easier to postpone, will
be come more infrequent over time, and eventually will go away.

These meetings can and should be brief and to the point. Work up a set
agenda and use it every time. Each member should probably contribute
to the information you'll review.

So, what is reviewed and discussed at these meetings? The vital business
information that is needed to keep the company moving toward its goals.

There is a separate chapter on key performance indicators. Pick the ones
that you feel you should monitor closely and bring those – freshly
updated - to each meeting. If some are out of whack, the team should
decide whether it's a trend or just a hiccup. You might choose to watch it
for another week or two, or to spring into action and do something about
it. These are all management decisions you make on a case-by-case
basis.

Management team meetings are a vehicle for monitoring progress on
your annual plan. Look at financial measures, projects and tasks that are
in the works, and individual accountabilities toward all of those. Hold
people accountable, congratulate progress, and make adjustments if
needed.

I like to use part of these meetings for department heads to notify the rest
of the management team about positive and negative issues, new
customers gained, lost customers, significant things going on in various
departments, issues with vendors, over budget, under budget, major
collection problems with specific customers, employee marriages, births,
deaths, promotions ... anything of substance and significance that
management team members need to know about.

Major issues for discussion that will take a significant amount of time
should be put on the agenda for a future meeting. This way, everyone
knows in advance to schedule extra time and can gather information and
prepare for this discussion.

None of this should take a long time. You should be able to run through the key performance indicators with some discussion in about 15 minutes. A quick update on company and department issues by all team members should also take another 10-15 minutes. If there are specific issues to be discussed at length, of course that adds time but it's doubtful you'll have these at every meeting.

In most companies, you should be able to knock out a management team meeting in 30 minutes flat. If you find these meetings dragging themselves out to an hour on a regular basis, you probably need to do a better job of reeling in discussions. Or not. If you feel that the discussions you're having are really substantive and valuable, that's fine. But be a tough judge and don't waste time. Like so much of the information in this book, tailor your approach to your business.

Management Team Strategic Planning Meetings

Your management team will need to spend considerable time each year developing a business plan for next year. Don't skimp on the time you allot for this critical activity.

Several half-day sessions may be needed, along with numerous shorter meetings. Some companies – even small ones – have an annual "management retreat" where the team members get away for a couple of days to work on their annual plan. However you choose to do it, make this part of your annual schedule.

Company-wide and Departmental Meetings

Your success depends largely on keeping your employees interested, informed, involved and engaged. Meetings can help.

Once per month seems to me a reasonable frequency to gather employees – either in each department or company-wide, depending on your size – for 15-30 minutes of training, informing, gathering feedback and celebrating. (If you practice open book management – which you should, at least on some level – more frequent meetings may be appropriate.) While you can always bring folks up to date on company news via email, some issues are best heard direct from the horse's mouth. And, these meetings are a good time and place for morale-building activities like celebrating employee birthdays or years of service.

At the department level, issues specific to that department can be tackled, such as productivity measures, workload, overtime schedules, quality issues, etc.

Brainstorming and Problem-Solving Meetings

Done right, these can really help move your company forward. Here are some guidelines:
- One person acts as facilitator to keep the meeting in order and moving forward.
- Clearly and specifically define the goal of the meeting.
- Everyone contributes.
- Every idea gets written down on a wipe-off board or flip chart.
- Don't dig into specifics or get bogged down discussing the details or merits of a specific idea. Just write it down and move on.
- Once the boss voices an opinion on an issue, the discussion on that issue is effectively over. This is a good time for the boss to stay in the background.

Once all the ideas and comments have been gathered, they you can go back through them and begin discussing, combining and eliminating them. Keep at it, and you should reach consensus on a course of action.

Other meetings

People can get be very inventive at coming up with reasons to hold meetings. Don't stifle creativity, but also don't allow meeting for the sake of meeting. Insist that your staff justifies their meetings and provides evidence of results.

How to run an effective meeting

Have you ever participated in a meeting that rambled aimlessly and strayed from its agenda (if it even had an agenda), was boring, seemed to go on forever, and produced few if any real results?

I'm going to share some tips with you, so you can inject order and structure into your meetings, get more done in less time, and most importantly – produce real, tangible results.

This information is, like everything else in this book, directed at small businesspersons. However, my tips on running effective meetings may also be applied to any meetings in which you're involved: school boards, volunteer organizations, and so on. Here we go ...

If you're running the show, your job actually starts several days before the meeting. Some of the things you need to do include:

- Confirm that all invited participants know about the meeting and its purpose
- Ensure that an agenda is prepared and if appropriate, circulate it to the participants prior to the meeting
- Ensure that your meeting room is available and set up the way you need it

If someone plans to make a presentation or give a report at your meeting, find out how much time he or she needs. Do not show up at the meeting only to be surprised when your speaker has a 45 minute slideshow and you only planned on a 30 minute meeting. Remember that you're not a passive bystander. You're in charge of getting this meeting started and ended on time. So, don't be afraid to ask a speaker to cut back on the time they want. But give the presenter the courtesy of doing it well in advance of the meeting.

Get to the meeting early. Check out the room, and make sure all your materials are in place. Start on time.

Pass out the agenda and use it to move through the meeting business. Be sure someone is assigned the important task of taking minutes or keeping notes.

Here are some things the person in charge should do during the meeting:

- Stay on topic. If a person starts to stray from the agenda, bring it back on course.
- Squelch side conversations. At any given time, the person speaking deserves the undivided attention of all involved.
- Prevent anyone from monopolizing the discussion.
- Pull in participants who aren't saying much. Ask for input and opinions from each individual.
- Watch your time. Make mid-meeting adjustments if necessary.

So you get through the meeting and it's about to end. You just adjourn and leave, right? Wrong! I strongly recommend that if any important decisions were made that call for follow-up action by folks at the meeting, you recap. Restate those actions and get a quick confirmation that these folks understand that they are accountable and have a timeframe for action.

For example: "Here are the commitments from today's meeting. Jack will write his report by next Friday, and Steve will visit our top 3 accounts by the end of the month. Right, Jack and Steve?" Getting people to acknowledge accountability in front of others is a powerful way to get them to actually keep their commitments.

I urge you to establish specific follow-up actions and timeframes. If Mary says, "I will work on the marketing plan", what does that mean? Can you hang your hat on that? A much better commitment might be: "I will get the marketing plan first draft written and submitted for review by May 1st."

Bottom line: If the follow-up action isn't deliverable, if it isn't measurable, if it isn't specific – you don't really have a commitment. Insist on specific actions by specific people by a specific date, and you will see results.

I know I'm putting a great deal of emphasis on accountability. Here's why: Everyone's busy, with lots of irons in the fire, both at work and in their personal lives. Many people have good intentions, and are great at making promises but not so good at follow-through.

You may be in charge of the meeting, but perhaps not in charge of the folks making these commitments. Away from work for instance, in a service club or volunteer organization setting, you have no real control over the meeting participants.

When people know others are watching, and others are counting on them, they'll follow through. Someone's word is a powerful thing. So is peer pressure. In some cases, these may be the only leverage you have to ensure results.

Finally, I like after-meeting emails to all participants to summarize the outcome and once again reconfirm the personal accountabilities and timeframes that were assigned.

If you follow these simple guidelines, your meetings will produce better results in less time.

"Our meetings have an agenda; we stay on topic; decisions are documented including who will do what by when." Can you honestly make this statement?

18. Mind your business: Key Performance Indicators

"We monitor a set of Key Performance Indicators, and use these to help make decisions."

I have personally met small business owners who don't look at their financial results until the end of the year, when they take a box of receipts to their accountant. A month or so after the year ends, they find out how they did.

I know others who can't tell you the difference between an income statement and a balance sheet. Some of these folks make key business decisions based solely on how much money is in the bank.

It's not my intent to belittle these folks. If anything, I hope they read this, see how they're limiting themselves and their businesses, and do something about it.

The language of business is numbers. Business owners must have a strong grasp of their numbers, they must be able to read, interpret and explain financial statements, and they must know how the various statements relate to each other.

If you don't have this level of understanding, I *strongly* recommend you sign up for an introductory accounting class at your local community college. You don't have to be in pursuit of a degree. In fact, most schools will let you "audit" their classes, meaning you're taking it for self-enrichment and not for a real grade. If that isn't available, consider an adult education or continuing education class on accounting. However you gain the information ... do it!

Monitoring financial indicators like revenue, gross profit, net profit, assets, liabilities and cash flow is a good start. But each business has its own unique set of Key Performance Indicators that should also be monitored. Some are financial and some are not.

Like keeping score in sports or using the cockpit gauges of an aircraft, you should continuously monitor what's going on while it's happening.

Cash is King

We're going to talk about all kinds of business measures in this chapter, but I'm asking you to keep this one bit of advice in mind at all times:

DON'T RUN OUT OF CASH!

If you run out of cash, it's over. All other measures pale in comparison.

Raw data versus information

Let's pause here to make a distinction between data and information. *Data* consists of raw numbers. By themselves, they are of some use but don't tell you everything you need to know. *Information* goes beyond the data. It might include a ratio, might indicate whether the data is on an upward or downward trend, and could include the story behind the numbers. *Information is data in context.* Here are some simple examples:

Data	Information
Revenue is $1,200,000	Revenue is $1,200,000, which is an increase of 8% over prior year, and is $50,000 over target..
Our freight expense last year was $13,000	Our freight expense was out of control last year. The previous year it had only been $5,500. Drastic changes are needed to bring it under control.
Employee turnover was 12% last year	Our employee turnover last year was 12%, but the average for our industry is 18%. Therefore, our turnover is low compared to similar companies in our industry.
Cash on hand is $700,000	Cash on hand 12 months ago was $450,000. Our collections initiatives have paid off.

Figure 18-1

Make every effort to get usable business *information*, and not just *data*.

What to monitor?

You drive your car looking through the windshield a lot more than you look in the rearview mirror. Yet, most small businesses are driven by looking in the rearview mirror almost exclusively. I'm talking about your financial statements, which give rear-looking information.

Don't get me wrong ... your financials are important. Vitally important. They show you whether you made a profit, how much cash you have on hand, and dozens of other measures of business performance.

But as good and important as they are, financials don't do a good job of predicting *future* results. OK, they can play a role in projecting ahead. If your revenue last January was $250,000 and sales are generally up about 3% every month since then, you may be safe projecting a 3% increase for next January.

But what if changes are in the picture ... employee turnover, lost major customers, or an increase or reduction in your marketing activities? As you make decisions and create budgets, it would be nice to have information that helps you make predictions about the future. That's where forward-looking measures come into play. These are simply financial and non-financial indicators of future results.

Examples of forward-looking indicators:
- If employee turnover is up, you can expect it to negatively impact the business
- If customer satisfaction is up, you can expect it to positively impact the business
- If your company has made a significant investment in training, you should expect a productivity improvement.
- A larger-than-usual marketing effort should bring in new sales.

This is not a precise science. You can't equate a 10% increase in your marketing budget to a 10% increase in sales. Nor can you predict a specific productivity increase from a training investment. Even so, a solid argument can be made for monitoring forward-looking indicators. Most of the strategic planning work you'll do is based on predictions and projections. These are educated guesses of future results. Why not throw

all available information into the mix and make some *really* educated
guesses?

In Figure 18-2, the Financial Measures are rear-looking, while the
Customer and Employee Measures are forward-looking. Granted, these
"forward-looking" measures really measure past performance, just like
your financials. But *unlike* financials, they *also* predict future
performance. You might say they *directly* measure past results while
indirectly predicting future results.

Key Performance Indicator Report for XYZ, Inc. For Month Ended:			
Measure	Actual	Target	Same Period Last Year
Financial Measures			
Revenue			
Cost of Goods Sold			
Gross Profit			
Compensation Expense			
Overhead Expense			
Net Profit Before Tax			
Current Ratio			
Cash on Hand			
Accounts Receivable Days			
Customer Measures			
Customer Satisfaction			
Major Account Retention			
Employee Measures			
Employee Satisfaction			
Training			
Employee Turnover			

Figure 18-2

This idea of supplementing financial metrics (metrics is another word for
measures) with other indicators is commonly called the "Balanced
Scorecard" system. Originated by two professors around 1990, this basic
system has been adopted and adapted by companies of all sizes. It has
also been the subject of a number of business books.
The "official" Balanced Scorecard consists of four business perspectives:

- The Learning and Growth Perspective
- The Business Process Perspective
- The Customer Perspective
- The Financial Perspective

While I offer some suggestions about what measures to monitor on a regular basis, don't let me or anyone else convince you that they have a one-size-fits-all answer. As you and your team go through various strategic planning activities, you have to decide what indicators are critical to your success.

Don't just measure something because you can. Ask yourself these questions:
- Can I describe, in a single sentence, what this indicator measures, why we need to know, and its impact on the business?
- If the number or indicator is off target, can we do anything specific to bring it back on track?

Carefully choose a few (about 15-20 maximum) Key Performance Indicators that paint a well-rounded picture of your past, present and future performance.

From among your key performance indicators, consider singling out one main metric for more attention than the rest. Jack Stack calls this your Critical Number. Jim Collins, author of mega best selling business book *Good to Great*, calls this the number that drives your economic engine. Whatever you call it, this is your single best measure of success, and you want everyone in your organization to pay attention to it.

Key Performance Indicators for Start-up Companies

For small start-up businesses, keep your monitoring system very simple. At this stage, the most important thing is to develop good habits – including running your business "by the numbers" and not just by gut reaction. Your system can and should evolve as your business grows. Start-up businesses should consider the information shown in Figure 18-3 as the minimum:

Information	Weekly	Monthly	Quarterly	Annually
Revenue by product/service/ customer categories *(Monitor DAILY if at all possible!)*	X	X	X	X
Cost of Goods Sold		X	X	X
Gross Profit Margin		X	X	X
Overhead expenses		X	X	X
Cash Flow	X	X	X	X
Accounts Receivable	X	X	X	X
Net Profit Before Tax (NPBT)		X	X	X
Inventory		X	X	X
Key Ratios as appropriate		X	X	X

Figure 18-3

How to monitor?

OK, so we've selected and set up our Key Performance Indicators. Now what?

Despite all I've written about Key Performance Indicators, you still need to review your raw financial statements: Income statement, balance sheet and cash flow statement. You certainly cannot ignore them. Look for numbers that are out of the norm, missing amounts, and generally be satisfied that all is in good order. But don't agonize over the statements or over individual entries. If you've done a good job of selecting your key performance indicators, they will keep you on the straight and narrow. The financials and your key performance indicators supplement each other to give you both a good overall view of your operation.

I recommend using three approaches to monitoring your key performance indicators. They are:
- Benchmarking
- Exception Management ("Red Flags")
- Trends

Benchmarking is a fancy word for "comparing." It's a good idea to benchmark your performance to see how you're doing. For instance, you may think that your 3% annual revenue growth is pretty good. But if everyone else in your industry – or your direct competitor down the street - is going gangbusters, growing at 10%+ per year, suddenly your results don't seem so hot.

You can and should have both internal and external benchmarks.

Internal benchmarks compare your own results from one period to another. The best example of this is your financial statement. It is common practice to have two columns on an income statement or balance sheet – This Year and Last Year. This form of internal benchmarking lets you quickly analyze whether this year is as good as or better than last year. The column headed "Same Period Last Year" in figure 18-2 is another example.

External benchmarks compare your results to those of your peers. A "peer" organization might be one of similar size, in the same industry, in your geographic area, or all of the above. The more a comparison company looks like yours, the more valid the comparison. Trade and industry associations are a good source for benchmarking information. So is information from publicly-traded companies.

Another way to get it: ask. Let's say you own a sporting goods store, and you read an article about a successful sporting goods retailer. Assuming that store is not in your town and thus not a direct competitor, the owner is likely to share information like revenue per employee, gross margins, and more. You can use this to gauge your own performance. (You could also get benchmarking information from publicly-traded sporting goods operations like Sports Authority. This may be interesting and of some value, but should be approached with caution. If you're a small business, such comparisons with huge companies have little validity for you.)

Exception management is the practice of setting up "Red Flags" – high and low marks for each important metric. Stay between them, and all is well. Stray on the negative side and corrective action is required. Exceed the red flag on the positive side and it's cause for celebration.

Exception management gives you freedom. It allows you to run your business without agonizing over every small change in your numbers. Instead of worrying whether a 1% swing in gross margin is significant, just see whether 1% is within your "red flag" zone. If so, move on to other things.

Where do "red flags" come from? You decide which measures deserve such treatment and where to set the boundaries. You do this during your strategic planning process. Benchmarking plays a large role in setting your red flags.

Trends are noteworthy, whether or not a measure is within its red flag zone. Keep track of the trends of your key performance indicators so you can capitalize on positive changes in a timely manner, and head off negative ones before they turn into trouble.

The Numbers and Open Book Management

Creating a "transparent" company and practicing OBM is largely about *the numbers*. The chapter on Communication deals with *how* to share numbers with your people. For now, let's discuss *which* numbers to share.

The whole idea behind the selection of key performance indicators is to dilute the myriad numbers, measures and ratios down to a manageable few that can be readily monitored by you and your leadership team.

Whether you're practicing OBM or simply giving your employees the information they need to do their jobs better, I recommend that you really zero in on which numbers are needed, depending on the department, the people, and the circumstances. Get even more selective based on relevance and importance. The information should be more and more focused as you get "closer to the action." Sometimes, less is more.

Here are some examples:
- If your sales team is tracking quotes and revenue, don't bog them down with data about manufacturing overhead. It might be nice to know, but it is not directly relevant to their sales efforts. Making such information available is good, but hanging it on the wall in an area where it will add to information clutter is not.
- You may have a company-wide meeting once a month to review financial results. "Big picture" numbers should be shown in this setting. Individual expense line items on the income statement probably should be ignored unless

something is particularly noteworthy and in need of discussion.

"We monitor a set of Key Performance Indicators, and use these to help make decisions." Can you honestly make this statement?

19. Information and Communication: There's almost no such thing as too much.

"All employees have ready access to all needed information. Ample communication flows in all directions."

In the movie *Liar, Liar*, Jim Carrey plays an attorney who can't lie for 24 hours, due to a wish made by his son. Predictably (and in my opinion, hilariously), uncontrollable honesty overtakes him and he says things he never would have said otherwise.

This is one of the few examples of too much communication that comes to my mind.

Information without communication is a waste of computer disk space and paper.

Communication without information is useless chatter.

Information and communication, combined, are the lifeblood of your business. Your job is to keep it flowing.

Happily, it's easy to do. We have so many high-tech communication options today it's almost ridiculous. And, of course, we still have good old face-to-face personal interaction ... for which there's no substitute.

I must admit that the title of this chapter is somewhat tongue in cheek. Of course you can have too much information and communication. It seems like everyone in the world is trying to communicate with us all day, every day. We're bombarded by information from all directions.

But the information I'm talking about here is information related to and useful to your business. The communication I'm referring to is business communication flowing into, out of, and through your company.

Part of optimizing information and communication in your company is cutting out the extraneous, low-value stuff. Then, determine who needs to know what information when. Finally, use the appropriate communication means to make it happen. And, everyone in your organization needs to be on board with this program.

Cutting down on low-value information and "communication"

I put communication in quotation marks because if it's of little value to your business, it really isn't communication. It's probably hollow drivel ... at least trivial and at worst, detrimental.

Here is a list of some of the things you can do to reduce the flow of low-value information in and around your business:

Email
- Install SPAM filtering software
- Implement a policy: Company computers and email are for business use only
- Nobody gives out email addresses to would-be junk emailers ... sweepstakes websites and the like
- Unsubscribe from unwanted email newsletters and email solicitations
- Forbid the receipt and forwarding of email chain letters, jokes, etc.

Mail
- Sort your mail over the trash can. Be ruthless!
- Call, write, fax or email to be taken off mail lists
- Cancel unnecessary magazine subscriptions, whether free or not

Fax
- Call, write, fax or email to be taken off fax broadcast lists
- Report junk fax violators to the proper authorities

Phone
- Have your calls screened (Do this with caution. Don't alienate your business contacts by making them jump through hoops to get to you.)
- Use voice mail. (Do this with caution. Don't alienate your business contacts by hiding behind voice mail.)

- Be direct when unwelcome solicitors call. Be professional but be firm. Tell them to put your company on their "Do Not Call" list, and then hang up. Don't feel obligated to listen to a sales pitch, to answer questions, or to engage in a conversation. Interrupt the caller if necessary.
- Strike a balance between being employee-friendly and too many personal calls. Here's a good guideline: Employees should make or receive no more than a couple of brief personal calls each day.
- See if you can sign up on "Do Not Call" registries. As of this writing, the national Do Not Call registry is only for personal numbers and not businesses. But many states have their own registries, so see if your state allows businesses to sign up.

Sending memos and forwarding various information items

- Only create memos when necessary
- Only send memos to employees who need them
- Only forward emails, faxes, mail, messages, magazines, voice mails, and other informational items to employees who need them

I used the words "necessary" and "need" in the list above. You'll have to decide what those words mean in your company. Some discussion and training will be in order to make sure everyone is on the same sheet of music.

Get everyone in your business involved in filtering, reducing and eliminating low-value and no-value information and communication so you can focus on using genuine, valuable business information communication in the pursuit of your goals.

Who needs to know what when?

So, now that we've filtered out the blather and are left with (mostly) useful information, how do we determine who needs to know what when?

Here's a start: *Everybody* does not need to know *everything* all the time.

Common sense plays a large role here. Does the company president need to know the soda machine is empty? Probably not. But does the president need to know the bank account is empty? If there's a fire in the outdoor break area barbeque pit, it's not news. A fire in the stock room, however, is another story.

For every person and for every department, I suggest there are two "scales" to consider: "Need to Know" and "Urgency to Know."

The Need to Know Scale
This person or department ...

Must have the info   Could use the info   Doesn't need the info at all

<--->

The Urgency to Know Scale
If the info is needed, the person or department ...

Needs it right now   Needs it soon   Will need it someday

<--->

I'm not suggesting you formalize this and make every bit of info flow through a system like this before it gets into the right hands. But, consider using a model like the one above when discussing and doing training on the subjects of information and communication.

Just as in another chapter we talked about getting your people to adopt "root cause thinking" for problem-solving, they can also adopt "need to know"/"urgency to know" thinking for information and communication.

This type of thinking will help your folks make decisions about how and when to communicate. For instance, does a piece of information justify interruption of a meeting, or should it simply be filed away for future reference? The Need to Know/Urgency to Know scales can become the common language in your company so no matter who encounters business information, there's a fighting chance that it will be handled and communicated appropriately.

How should we communicate?

Honestly, openly, clearly, professionally and directly.

With whom should we communicate?

Everyone inside and outside the company, filtered through the "Need to Know" model: Employees, employees' families, shareholders, customers, suppliers, lenders, and the community.

What means should we use to communicate and share business information?

- Face-to-face one-on-one discussions – formal and informal, planned and unplanned
- Department and company meetings
- Training sessions – On-the-Job, formal, and impromptu
- Scoreboards and wall charts
- Bulletin boards, signs and banners
- Emails – to individuals, to departments and to the entire company
- Public web sites
- Private intranet sites
- Memos, notes and letters
- Phone calls, teleconferences and video conferences
- Faxes
- Reference files for future use – paper or electronic

(This chapter deals primarily with non-marketing communications, so I haven't included ads or other sales-related communications in this list.)

Make use of all the communications and information storing methods available to you. Mix it up.

Stubbornly refuse to use email and the web at your own peril.

Who is responsible for capturing and sharing information?

Everyone.

The company owns its information

Any and all business information discovered, captured, learned, taught, saved, printed, copied, broadcasted, conveyed, passed on, aggregated, assembled, collated, compiled, consolidated, accumulated, gathered, hoarded, amassed, shared, documented, filed, ascertained, caught, conceived, contrived, designed, detected, determined, devised, dug up, discerned, identified, invented, located, looked up, written down and/or communicated by your employees *belongs to the company*.

I touched on this in the chapter on Policies, Procedures and Systems. I'll repeat it again in the chapter on Continuous Improvement and Learning.

This is critical:

Do not let your company's knowledge base and know-how walk out the doors at quitting time each day.

Document and safeguard your business information. It is among your most precious possessions and likely represents the single biggest factor in determining the value of your business. Buildings and computers can be replaced. It may sound cold, but even employees can be replaced. The information inside frequently cannot.

The information in your own head needs to come out so you are not indispensable to the business, and so the business can rely on others. This is key for you to have a life outside your business.

The information in your employees' heads needs to come out so the business is not dependent on anyone. People change jobs. People win the lottery. People die unexpectedly. People go bad and embezzle.

"Document and safeguard your business information" doesn't mean to jealously hide information. As I've already established, I'm a proponent of open book management and information sharing. I'm convinced that the only path to true business success and having a life is through shared information and open communications.

But having an open-information environment doesn't mean being naive or foolish. Probably the best defense against problems is to surround yourself with good, honest people and treat them well. Many problems with disgruntled ex-employees can be blamed – at least in part – on the company. Hire "gruntled" people and then don't give them a reason to become disgruntled.

I contend that most business information – the stuff that makes a company efficient on a day to day basis, such as who is doing what, current company goals, and so on – is not sensitive information anyway.

Some business owners rely on non-compete/non-disclosure agreements. Depending on the situation and where you operate, these may or may not have any legal teeth. Even so, their mere existence may deter some folks from bad behavior.

Here are some tips to operate safely in an open-information environment:

- Follow good accounting practices and principles. Make sure you have paper trails, audit trails, and other safeguards in place. The person who does the purchasing should not also pay the bills. Have a CPA help you set up your system.
- Use the "Need to Know" model. Share information where it needs to be shared, but don't post things in public locations if you're concerned about it being seen by the wrong people.
- Properly dispose of sensitive documents.
- Use passwords on computers and networks.
- Document as much as possible. Critical business processes and other knowledge needs to be recorded and not just in someone's brain – no matter how much you trust the person.

"All employees have ready access to all needed information. Ample communication flows in all directions." Can you honestly make this statement?

20. Continuous Improvement and Learning

"I am committed to Continuous Improvement and Learning for both myself and the company."

A little girl is in the kitchen, watching her mom prepare dinner. Her mom cuts both ends off the ham and places it carefully in the baking pan.

"Why do you cut the ends off the ham, mom?" asks the girl.

"I've always done it that way. I learned it from your grandmother when I was your age."

"I'm really curious about it. Do you mind if I call Grandma and ask her about it?"

"Not at all, honey. Go ahead."

So the little girl gets Grandma on the phone. "Hi, Grandma. Do you know how you always cut the ends off the ham before you put it in the pan?"

"That's right, dear. I always cut the ends off."

"Why do we do that?"

"I've always done it that way. I learned it from your great-grandmother when I was your age."

"I'm really curious about it. Do you mind if I call Great-Grandma and ask her about it?"

"Not at all, dear. Go ahead."

So the little girl gets Great-Grandma on the phone. "Hi, Great-Grandma. Do you know how you always cut the ends off the ham before you put it in the pan?"

"Oh, sweetie, I haven't done that in years."

"Why not, Great-Grandma?" asks the girl.

"Because they make the pans bigger nowadays."

Is your organization "cutting the ends off the ham" without even thinking about it? The worst reason for doing something a certain way is "We've always done it this way."

Continuous Improvement

The concept of "continuous improvement" means just what it says – ongoing, daily improvement. It can be used by people and by organizations.

Here are two mantras for you to consider adopting
- "Better than yesterday"
- "Challenge everything"

Let's explore these slogans.

"Better than yesterday" is a heck of a good goal for all of us to shoot for, isn't it? Some folks work in a job for ten years and have ten years of experience. Other folks work in a job for ten years and have one year of experience, ten times. Growing and getting better every day takes some effort. You have to fight through the hustle, bustle and clamor of the workday. You have to train and discipline yourself to pay attention ... to recognize improvement opportunities when you encounter them, and then to stop and do something about them. When people and organizations – individually and collectively – really, truly, genuinely commit themselves to the goal of "better than yesterday", great things happen. I've seen it firsthand.

"Challenge everything." It sounds like something that might have been said by a long-haired guy wearing a headband back in the 1960s. Think of the ham story. Instead of clinging to old ways, people and organizations should challenge the way everything is done, every day. Just because it was done that way last week doesn't mean it's right for us this week. I'm not suggesting you jettison existing approaches on a wholesale basis. I am suggesting that you and your people at least challenge them. Put them to the test and make sure they are still appropriate for today's goals, plans, people, environment, marketplace and situations. It would be irresponsible to run around pulling the plug on proven techniques, endorsing change for the sake of change. But, it's just as irresponsible to hang onto old methods without being open to new ways and improvement.

If your company is new, this stuff is pretty easy. Adopt these outlooks from the start. Make it part of your culture.

If your company has been around for quite a few years, and if you have long-term employees, it might be tougher. Change is not easily embraced by some people, so take your time and avoid shocking the troops. Move slowly, move gently, but be firm. Change is inevitable, and ultimately you'll have to insist that everyone get on board and support changes as they occur.

So, where do improvement ideas come from? Everywhere. And, from everyone.

I love the concept of "best practices." This is a polite way to describe ideas borrowed from someone else. Essentially, you find out what works for someone else – either inside your company or in other organizations – and then adopt the approach.

No matter what business problem you're trying to solve - or what business process you're trying to improve – there's a good chance someone else has already tackled it and has come up with a good solution. Why reinvent the wheel?

By the way, this is not covert industrial espionage I'm talking about. Entrepreneurs, for the most part, are open, helpful folks who will share tips with you ... as long as you're not a competitor. Ask someone how they did something, and they'll probably take the time to tell you.

Your employees are a terrific source of ideas and improvements. (You don't really believe you have the market cornered on brainpower or good ideas, do you?) Tap into this resource. Ask for ideas. Take them seriously. Implement them. Celebrate them. Reward for them. Make a big deal of it when someone comes up with a good idea or an improvement. Most importantly – *give the employee the credit for his or her idea.* Don't let anyone else take credit or steal the limelight from the employee.

So, is a formal system needed to mine these ideas? It's up to you and your company's culture. The old suggestion box on the wall seems to have fallen from favor, probably because management didn't give feedback, credit and thanks for ideas.

Whether or not you implement a formal system for suggesting improvements, make sure you put a high value on small ideas and small improvements. If your folks are waiting to come up with an idea that will save ten thousand dollars a year, you won't get many ideas. Big ideas are few and far between. Little ideas are everywhere. Focus on the small, incremental changes that, over time, add up to significant improvement.

Learning

We've all heard the old saying "You learn something new every day" a million times. It's probably true. In fact, I hope it is.

Despite the natural curiosity possessed by most entrepreneurs, it's so easy to get bogged down running a business and to put off proactive activities like learning. To use Stephen Covey's words, to let the urgent displace the important.

We talked in the previous section about Best Practices. How can you learn about someone else's good ideas unless you pry yourself away from your desk, get outside your four walls and see what the heck is going on elsewhere? Answer: you can't.

Throughout this book, I've made note of things that, if not done, will limit your company's potential. I suggest that ongoing learning, if not done, will limit *your* potential as a business owner. It will limit your ability to effectively run and grow your company, and it will limit your ability to have a life outside your business.

Since you bought my book and are reading it (thank you), I may be preaching to the choir. Perhaps you've already bought into the idea of life-long learning. If so, congratulations. If not, this is my challenge to you: Make learning part of your life.

I further challenge you to make learning part of your company's culture. Encourage it, both on and off the job. Make time for it. Celebrate it. Facilitate it.

There are so many opportunities for both formal and informal learning and education that finding the time to do it almost becomes less daunting than sorting through the opportunities to find the ones of most value.

Folks in the business world need to stay abreast of a variety of topics. These include technical/trade/skill training and continuing education, general business, and your industry. I like to throw in some occasional motivational stuff for good measure.

Work on developing a well-rounded base of general business knowledge. The topics are almost limitless: taxes, government regulations, motivating employees, financial analysis, worker compensation insurance, computers, commercial real estate, health insurance, depreciation ... you get the idea. I'm not suggesting that you try to become an expert in all these areas. It's neither practical nor necessary. But some amount of knowledge in a broad range of topics applicable to your business is highly advisable. As we've discussed in this book, the goal is to work *on* your business rather than *in* your business. In other words, you don't want to remain the primary widget-maker. To grow beyond that role requires knowledge beyond the core technical work done by your company.

I personally have always considered industry trade journals to be among the best training materials available. First of all, most are free subscriptions. In them, you'll find ads from both suppliers and competitors (so you can find out who's out there and what they're up to), "how-to" articles, industry news, new product releases, and much more. Many of these journals conduct annual salary surveys, so you can compare your compensation strategy to others in your industry.

I'm a big believer in listening to cassette tapes and CDs while you drive. All the motivational speakers have recordings, and most business books are available in audio format. Music and talk radio are great, and I listen to both. But when I take a road trip of more than 45 minutes or so, I bring business and motivational recordings with me. What a great use of time.

Here is a list of just some of the learning and educational opportunities
for you and your people:

- Books
- Audio books
- Web sites
- Email newsletters and reports
- Trade journals and magazines
- Business magazines
- Industry trade shows and conferences
- One-day seminars (like SkillPath, Fred Pryor, etc.)
- Lunchtime educational meetings (chamber of commerce, etc.)
- Toastmasters International (Speaking/presentation training - chapters all over the world)
- Public libraries
- Community college for-credit classes
- Community college adult/continuing education classes
- Formal classes designed and presented by your employees, held at your place of business
- Formal classes by outside trainers, held at your place of business
- Informal, impromptu OJT (on-the-job training)
- Self-paced/self-taught courses that you design
- Self-paced/self-taught courses that you buy
- Learn from other businesspersons – take them to lunch, pay for a round of golf ... whatever it takes.

I ate at an all-you-can-eat buffet one time with a sign that said, *"If you
leave hungry, it's your own fault."* With all these educational
opportunities available, we could just as easily say, *"If you don't engage
in lifelong learning, it's your own fault."*

I went into some detail on this in the chapter on Information and
Communication, so I'll only mention this in passing as a reminder:
Information and training materials developed by or paid for by your
company belong to the company. Don't spend time and money working
up training materials and other information unless you intend to integrate
it into your company's base of knowledge. Yes, you want individuals to
learn, but more importantly you want *the company* to learn.

Open Book Management and business literacy training

I've talked about OBM in a number of chapters. Hopefully, you're sold on the idea of creating a transparent company. If so, one of the keys is business literacy training.

It should be self-evident that sharing information won't work unless the employees know what they're looking at. Opening the books is just the start. An OBM environment is characterized by ongoing education about the numbers ... what they mean, how they interact, how each employee impacts the numbers, and so on.

If you take the time to teach your employees not just about their jobs, but also about the business, the payback can be enormous. Just so nobody thinks I'm sugar-coating this, let me be clear: It's hard work. It takes lots of time and effort. Some of your employees won't buy in, and they'll resist.

But, if you push through the obstacles, are committed, and create a company of *businesspeople* all focused on a common goal ... you'll be a force to be reckoned with.

"I am committed to Continuous Improvement and Learning for both myself and the company." Can you honestly make this statement?

Epilog: A week in the life of a successful small business owner who actually has a life ... *This could be you!*

Bob is the founder and president of Bob's Printing Company, Inc. Bob learned the printing business during ten years running a press for a large family-owned printing company. When his former company was sold to an out-of-town buyer, Bob lost his job. He figured, "Hey, I know how to run a printing press. Why not be my own boss?" And so Bob's Printing Company was born. Bob was smart enough to know he didn't have all the answers, and he knew plenty of small business owners – many of whom didn't seem particularly happy or successful. So he made a commitment to learn all he could about running a business. He reached out to his successful friends for advice, got hooked up with a business coach, attended educational small business conferences, and read as many books and articles as he could get his hands on.

Monday June 29:

Bob is frequently the first to arrive. He's a morning person, and he loves to get to the office early, grab a cup of coffee, and get started. Today is no exception. As he unlocks the doors at 7:00AM, he looks around. Even though his business is in its fifth year, he still has the same feelings of excitement and anticipation when he opens up. His name is on the building and everything in the place is his – the furniture, the printing presses, the computers – even the pens in the drawers.

Last Monday had been a big day. His main press operator who has been with Bob since day one, Jeff, was promoted to Production Manager. The business had grown to the point that Bob could no longer handle production scheduling. Today, Jeff will join the Management Team for the first time in their weekly meeting. Jeff had been the obvious choice. His recommendations for improvement had streamlined the printing operation and saved days of turnaround time, and the other press operators looked up to him.

The promotion created an opening for a press operator. Bob had collaborated with Jeff to write a "help wanted" ad, which ran in yesterday's paper, so Bob expects to start receiving resumes early this week.

Bob makes his way to his desk. Bob turns on his computer so he can check his email. Not much there – typical for early Monday. He has one informational email from his chamber of commerce, which he flags to read later. He makes a pot of coffee and sits down to review his schedule for the week.

Next, Bob looks over the agenda for today's Management Team meeting. These usually last about 30 minutes, but today he wants to allow extra time to give Jeff a thorough orientation to the team meetings.

The employees trickle in, and shortly after 8:00, Bob starts his weekly routine of walking through each department. He likes to make small talk with the employees and see if anything needs his attention.

Promptly at 9:00, the management team is ready to start their weekly meeting in the conference room. The team consists of Joan in accounting, Sally, the sales person, Roger from the artwork department, and now Jeff.

Bob opens the meeting. "Good morning. I'm pleased and proud to welcome Jeff to the management team. Let's get started."

The team has an agenda they use every week. It starts with a review of the Key Performance Indicator report, which includes metrics on all aspects of the business: sales, gross margin, overhead expenses, profit, cash, receivables, customer satisfaction survey results, and more.

Sally comments on the sales results. "We're about 5% over our year to date target through May, and although we haven't finished June yet, I predict that we'll finish the first two quarters right on target or slightly above. But, the big catalog printing job we do for Brewster every June has been postponed to July. So, by the end of July we should be at least 8% ahead of our plan." There are a few questions posed to Sally, but everyone agrees with her revenue assessment.

The team sees that net profit before tax is strong – well ahead of last year and also ahead of plan. A brief discussion is held about the implications. Even without the Brewster job in June, the company wide bonus target will almost certainly be exceeded – resulting in nice bonus checks for all.

Roger speaks up. "You may be wondering why I budgeted $3500 for the year for computer upgrades, but haven't spent the money. We'll be doing this in August, when a new version of their design software gets released."

Joan leads a review of the receivables. "We have only 6% of total receivables older than 60 days – a new record for us." Joan is congratulated for her department's work on keeping receivables in line. There are a couple of hard-to-collect accounts, so Sally offers to call these clients to see if she can help.

Bob then describes his transition plan for Jeff. "Jeff will begin to track the production metrics that I have been handling. I'll be working with him to ensure a smooth transition, and also on hiring a new press operator. As usual, candidates invited back for a second visit will undergo panel interviews. We'll let you know when to expect candidates."

He continues, "Our open-book management implementation seems to be going well. I attribute much of this year's success to it. Thanks, everyone, for spending the time to get up to speed yourselves and then working with the staff to make this work."

The meeting wraps up with further discussion about Jeff's training plan. The team agrees to a half-day meeting in mid-July to review their results for the first half of the year and to review their plans for the rest of the year. Bob lets the team know that he'll be out of the office this afternoon.

After the meeting, Bob spends the rest of the morning with Jeff. The two go out to lunch together and agree that Jeff will spend some time running his press until his replacement is hired, but should also start setting up his new office.

The two return to the office. Bob checks his email and his in-box. Satisfied that nothing urgent is pending, Bob leaves to meet his wife Abby at their daughter's school for an open house and parent-teacher meeting. Then, they'll take both kids out to dinner.

Once home, they tuck the kids into bed. With the kids asleep, Bob and Abby have time to talk. Bob starts. "Abby, things are going great at work. It looks like all the employees – me included – will be receiving mid-year bonus checks. I know when we decided to max out in the retirement program this year we worried that we were being too optimistic. But it's worked out wonderfully."

"I'm so proud of you, Bob. I must admit I was very nervous at first about taking out a loan and starting a new business. Your long hours that first year were hard on the family but it's all paying off now."

Tuesday June 30:

Bob starts the day in his office at 7:30AM. He has a dozen or so emails, and some need replies. He also has mail in his inbox - mostly junk mail - from yesterday, so he goes through it. No voice mails are waiting for him.

He then turns his attention to the company's intranet system, which Bob maintains himself. He sees that there are several employee suggestion program submittals waiting for him, so he reads them and responds to each.

At 9:30, the mail man arrives. Bob opens the mail and finds 12 resumes for the press operator job. He asks Jeff to join him in sorting through them. They both agree that 7 of the candidates have adequate qualifications for a phone interview. Bob reviews the company's hiring system with Jeff, which includes a standard set of questions for a screening phone interview and also for in-person interviews. Using the speaker phone, they manage to speak with 4 of the applicants. Using the phone interview form as a guide, they go through the series of questions and make written notes. Two of the four are granted in-person interviews, which are set up for 2:00 and 4:00 tomorrow. Bob sends an email to the rest of the management team to let them know about the candidates.

Bob is active in his local chamber of commerce, and today is the monthly lunch meeting. Either Bob or Sally try to attend most chamber meetings. Today, Sally is on appointments so Bob goes alone. He arrives early to do some networking.

Back at the office after lunch, Bob is elated to find an email message from Linda at Brewster Manufacturing, one of Bob's top customers. "I'm pleased to tell you that we've selected Bob's Printing Company as our Supplier of the Year. Congratulations." Bob forwards Linda's email to everyone in the company. In it, he adds his own message. He thanks them for their hard work and their commitment to outstanding service. He also tells his team how proud he is of them.

He spends the early part of the afternoon working on his plans for the management team's half-day July meeting. The rest of the afternoon is spent revamping the format of the customer satisfaction surveys the company sends out with every job. Bob heads out at 4:30 to meet Abby and the kids at the mall to shop for a new TV.

Wednesday July 1:

At 7:00 AM, Bob arrives. After routine work at his desk, he spends the rest of the morning training Jeff on the Key Performance Indicator report, how to get the metrics it contains, and what they all mean.

Bob meets Abby for lunch.

Back at the office, Bob finds 5 more resumes for the open position. He and Jeff again screen the resumes and conduct more phone interviews. A total of 5 in-person interviews are scheduled. Again Bob notifies the management team of the schedule. Then he and Jeff prepare for the two interviews they will conduct today.

The first applicant, Larry, arrives right at 2:00. Bob greets him, introduces him to Jeff, and asks him to fill out an application. When he's done, Bob and Jeff begin the interview process. Bob gives a brief introduction to the company, then they take turns asking questions from their interview form. Most questions are open-ended, and focus on character and behavior. Larry does the majority of the talking. When their questions are finished, Bob asks Larry if he has any questions. He is interested in the open book management that Bob mentioned in his introduction, so Bob explains further. Larry seems to like the sound of bonuses based on team performance.

The interview lasts about an hour. When done, Jeff gives Larry a tour of the facility and walks him out. Jeff returns to the conference room to compare notes with Bob. They go through the forms they completed and look for positives and negatives. Both men had a positive impression of Larry. "He seems like he'd be a good fit. He's clean-cut, polite, and his responses sure sound like he's big on customer service", offered Jeff. "I agree", replied Bob. "Plus, I really like the interest and enthusiasm he showed toward our open book management program."

Bob fills out the candidate evaluation form and approves him for a second interview – a "panel" interview with the entire management team and at least one person who would be the candidate's co-worker - pending the outcome of a background check.

The second candidate, Sam, arrives at 4:05, with no explanation for being late. The process goes just like the one with Larry. Sam has 15 years of press experience. For the last two years, Sam worked for Bob's largest local competitor, Smith Printing. When the subject of past employment comes up, Sam has little good to say about Smith and says he left over a dispute with his manager. When given the opportunity to ask questions, Sam's only interest is about pay and benefits.

Reviewing Sam's interview, it doesn't take Bob and Jeff long to reach the conclusion that Sam is not right for the company. "He arrived late without apologizing, bad-mouthed his previous employer, and just plain came across to me as unlikable", said Jeff. "You're right", agreed Bob. "We'll send him a 'thanks for your interest' letter and take him off our list."

Bob and Jeff finish their notes on the interviews. Bob scans tomorrow's schedule: One interview at 9:00 AM, a sales call and customer lunch with Sally at 11:00, and two more interviews in the afternoon, at 3:00 and 4:30 PM. He leaves the building at 5:15.

Thursday July 2:

On Thursday morning, Bob stops at the gym for his weekly workout. He gets to the office at 8:00. He checks his email and voice mail, and then prepares for his sales visit with Sally at the Hogan Company. Bob's has some business with Hogan but Sally reports there is much greater potential. She managed to get Jim Hogan, the company president, to agree to a meeting, so Bob is coming along so the two CEOs can get to know each other. Bob digs into Hogan's website, reviews Bob's past jobs for them, and pulls a Dun and Bradstreet report to prepare for their meeting. He finds Sally and gives the information to her to review. It's 9:00 – time for the interview.

Jeff and Bob conduct the interview, again using the standard format. After their post-interview meeting, Bob and Sally drive to Hogan's headquarters.

"Pretty impressive place", says Sally as they pull into the parking lot. "With 175 employees, I'm sure they're doing much more printing than we currently see from them."

Jim Hogan greets them in the lobby and takes them on a tour. Bob drives them to lunch at his favorite restaurant, where all three share a bit of personal information before getting down to business. Sally describes their design and printing capabilities, and then Bob talks with obvious pride about the company culture, their people, their systems, and briefly gives the history from start-up to present day. Bob thinks it's a good sign that Jim is taking notes.

In the car on the way back to the Hogan facility, Jim says, "Bob, I can tell you're proud of your company, and you should be. You're way ahead of the curve and are approaching things the right way. Personally, it took me many years of hard lessons before we got on the right track."

Jim continues, "Without naming names, I'll let you know that most of your competitors call on us. We've tried a number of them. Most come in here and try to get our business with a low-ball price but later can't deliver on their promises. And it's not just printers. We've seen it with our other vendors, too. So over the years, we've adopted a philosophy that says: we expect competitive pricing, but we also look to develop relationships with companies who share our values and who keep their promises to us. This allows us in turn to keep our promises to *our* customers. I like what you're told me. Let's make an appointment for my purchasing manager and me to tour your facility, and we'll see about a six month trial where we send you most of our printing business. If you pass the test – and I'll warn you that my purchasing manager can be tough – I see no reason why you couldn't become our primary printing vendor."

During the ride back to the office, Sally thanks Bob for joining her. She confides in him for the first time that it's nice to sell for a company she believes in. At her previous two sales jobs, she felt like one of the people Jim described: making promises she knew her company wouldn't keep. Sally says that the confidence she has in the company makes her job easier and more enjoyable.

After the long lunch meeting, Bob checks email and voice mail, cleans out the inbox on his desk, and visits briefly with Sally to compare schedules for the Hogan visit.

Bob and Jeff conduct their two interviews. The two men agree that they've got four strong candidates to send to the next stage of panel interviews.

Just as he's heading out the door at 5:45, he sees Joan also leaving. "Bob, I still have some work to do in the morning closing the June books, but as expected, we're over the top on our bonus plan."

"Great news, Joan!" exclaims Bob. Thanks for the update and thanks for staying to get this far along. I'll see you tomorrow."

Bob feels a sense of accomplishment. He can't wait to tell Abby the good news about Hogan and the company-wide bonus.

Friday July 3:

Arriving at 7:15 AM, Bob looks over his schedule for today. He has scheduled two hours this morning to work again with Jeff, this time going over the method Bob has been using to schedule printing jobs. And, Bob wants Jeff to start running his department's weekly meetings starting next week, so they discuss that change. They get done at 10:00.

Back at his desk, Bob finds the June financials. He looks them over and likes what he sees. He spends the next two hours preparing for next Wednesday's all-company meeting. They hold these meetings on the second Wednesday of every month, but this one will be special. The second quarter bonus will be announced. The first hour, Bob works on the agenda and lists various topics he wants to cover. Then Joan joins him and they calculate the bonuses. "By the way, I faxed our financials to Walter at the bank before I came in here", says Joan.

"Thanks, Joan, for getting the books closed so quickly. I think this is a new record."

Bob almost always sets aside time on Friday afternoons to review the past week and plan the next week. But this is the end of a quarter, and Bob schedules half a day with himself to review his personal goals, the business plan, and the prior quarter results and accomplishments. He takes lunch into his office and closes the door. Bob maintains an open-door policy but really looks forward to his quiet time alone.

Sitting back in his chair, Bob reflects on the past week, his business and his personal life. Time with his family. An award from a customer, and a potential new large customer. A salesperson with confidence in the company. A newly-promoted employee. Sales and profits are up. Bonuses for all. "Wow!" thinks Bob. "I'm living my dream."

Appendix A: The "How to Succeed as a Small Business Owner and Still Have a Life" Assessment

	Section 1 PURPOSE *Your business should serve you ... not the other way around.*	
1	I went into business because I'm passionate about my industry and about being an entrepreneur.	
2	I believe that my business exists to serve me and to enhance the lives of my family and myself.	
3	I pay myself first, and don't make undue personal sacrifices of time or money for the sake of the business.	
	Section 2 PREPARATION *If you don't know where you're going, any road will take you there.*	
4	I set goals that are specific, ambitious, achievable & balanced. I define tasks & action steps for each one.	
5	I have personal & family goals: long-term, short-term, retirement & multi-generational.	
6	I have business goals: long-term, short-term and an exit strategy. All are consistent with my personal goals.	
7	I have a written business plan with a vision, strategies, a budget & an action plan for achieving all these.	
8	I have written marketing plans and a marketing budget.	
9	I actively use my plans to run my business. I review them periodically & change course when appropriate.	

Section 3   EXECUTION
If you put in long hours, have trouble getting away from work for more than a day or two at a time, and don't make any more money than you did when you worked for someone else, you haven't created a business. You've created a job.

10	I make good use of time. I use a calendar, and I schedule personal time and planning time for myself.	
11	We have a written list of values, everyone knows them, and they truly guide our actions.	
12	We make sure to only hire the right people. If we don't know we've found the right candidate, we keep looking.	
13	We retain our employees using competitive pay & benefits, and via our positive, high-involvement culture.	
14	We use written Policies, Procedures, & Systems to ensure quality, consistency & to minimize "reinventing the wheel"	
15	We use a corrective action system to identify & fix the root cause of errors and to prevent future problems.	
16	I delegate authority & allow others the freedom to determine how to reach the desired results	
17	Our meetings have an agenda; we stay on topic; decisions are documented including who will do what by when.	
18	We monitor a set of Key Performance Indicators, and use these to help make decisions.	
19	All employees have ready access to all needed information. Ample communication flows in all directions.	
20	I am committed to Continuous Improvement and Learning for both myself and the company.	

Response Legend
5   Strongly agree
4   Agree
3   Neither agree nor disagree; don't know
2   Disagree
1   Strongly disagree

About the Author

Bill Collier is the president of Collier Business Advisors, LLC. He provides coaching, consulting, training and strategic planning services for small to mid-sized companies and their owners. A professional speaker, Bill offers speaking engagements and workshops for trade, business and other groups.

He is the founder and former president of BC Group International, Inc., a company which made the "St. Louis Technology Fast 50" list three times and which he sold in early 2005. In March 2005, Bill was given the "Hall of Fame" award by the Great Game of Business for "extraordinary business practices and performance."

Bill is active in a variety of community, business and non-profit organizations and is an active partner in a small manufacturing company in Kirkwood, Missouri.

Bill and his wife Joyce have been married since 1978. They have two grown daughters, Katie and Chrissy, and live in a suburb of St. Louis.

If you're interested in Bill's help with implementing any of the ideas in this book, or in having him speak to your organization, contact him at 314-221-8558 or bill@collierbiz.com.

Visit our website and sign up for Bill's monthly email newsletter:

www.CollierBiz.com

Let's put your business to work ... for you! SM

Business Coaching • Consulting • Strategic Planning • Speaking • Training

Printed in the United States
77920LV00006B/79-114